Street by Street

CW00393751

CREWE

ALSAGER, NANTWICH, SANDBACH

Barthomley, Elworth, Haslington, Hough, Ravensmoor, Rode Heath, Shavington, Weston, Wheelock, Willaston, Wybunbury

1st edition September 2002

© Automobile Association Developments Limited 2002

Ordnance Survey® This product includes map data licensed from Ordnance Survey® with the permission of the Controller of Her Majesty's Stationery Office. © Crown copyright 2002. All rights reserved. Licence No: 399221.

Published by AA Publishing (a trading name of Automobile Association Developments Limited, whose registered office is Millstream, Maidenhead Road, Windsor, Berkshire SL4 5GD. Registered number 1878835).

The Post Office is a registered trademark of Post Office Ltd. in the UK and other countries.

Schools address data provided by Education Direct.

One-way street data provided by:

Tele Atlas   © Tele Atlas N.V.

Mapping produced by the Cartographic Department of The Automobile Association. A01100

A CIP Catalogue record for this book is available from the British Library.

Printed by GRAFIASA S.A., Porto, Portugal

The contents of this atlas are believed to be correct at the time of the latest revision. However, the publishers cannot be held responsible for loss occasioned to any person acting or refraining from action as a result of any material in this atlas, nor for any errors, omissions or changes in such material. This does not affect your statutory rights. The publishers would welcome information to correct any errors or omissions and to keep this atlas up to date. Please write to Publishing, The Automobile Association, Fanum House (FH17), Basing View, Basingstoke, Hampshire, RG21 4EA.

Ref: ML197

Key to map pages	ii-iii
Key to map symbols	iv-1
Enlarged scale pages	2-3
Street by Street	4-41
Index – towns & villages	42
Index – streets	43-48
Index – featured places	48

ii

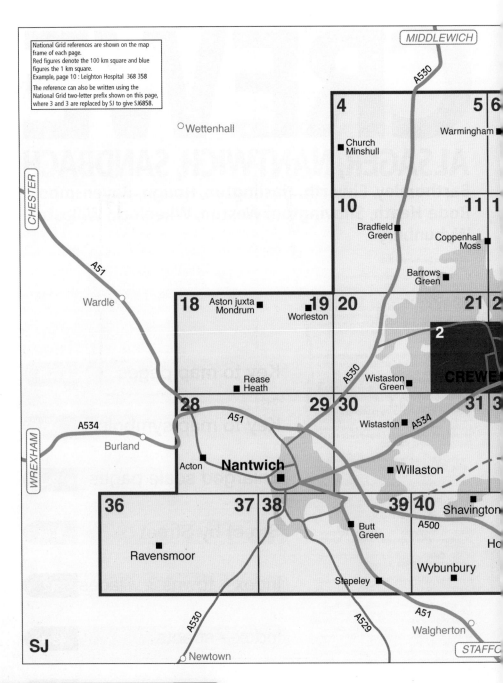

National Grid references are shown on the map frame of each page.
Red figures denote the 100 km square and blue figures the 1 km square.
Example, page 10 : Leighton Hospital 368 358

The reference can also be written using the National Grid two-letter prefix shown on this page, where 3 and 3 are replaced by SJ to give SJ6858.

MIDDLEWICH

A530

CHESTER

○ Wettenhall

4

■ Church Minshull

5 **6**

Warmingham ■

10

Bradfield ■ Green

11 **1**

Coppenhall ■ Moss

A51

Barrows ■ Green

Wardle ○

18   Aston juxta ■ Mondrum

19 **20**
■ Worleston

21 **2**

2

CREWE

A530

Rease ■ Heath

Wistaston ■ Green

28

A51

29 **30**

Wistaston ■   A534

31 **3**

WREXHAM

A534

Burland ○

Acton ■

Nantwich
■

Willaston ■

36

37 **38**

Ravensmoor ■

Butt ■ Green

39 **40**   Shavington ■

A500

Ho

Wybunbury ■

Stapeley ■

A530

A529

A51

Walgherton ○

SJ

STAFFO

Newtown ○

Enlarged scale pages   **1:10,000**   6.3 inches to 1 mile

0   1/4   miles   1/2
0   1/4   1/2   kilometres   3/4   1

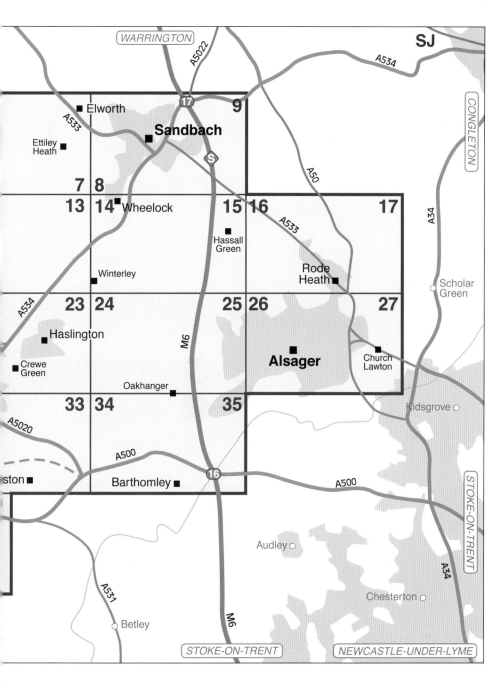

WARRINGTON
A5022
SJ
A534
CONGLETON
Elworth
A553
Sandbach
Ettiley Heath
17
9
S
A50
7 **8**
13 **14** Wheelock
15 **16**
A533
17
A34
Hassall Green
Winterley
Rode Heath
Scholar Green
A534
23 **24**
25 **26**
27
Haslington
M6
Alsager
Church Lawton
Crewe Green
Oakhanger
33 **34**
35
Kidsgrove
A5020
A500
Barthomley
16
A500
STOKE-ON-TRENT
ston
Audley
A531
A34
Chesterton
Betley
STOKE-ON-TRENT
NEWCASTLE-UNDER-LYME

4.2 inches to 1 mile   **Scale of main map pages** 1:15,000

0   1/4   miles   1/2   3/4   1
0   1/4   1/2   kilometres 3/4   1   1 1/4   1 1/2

Junction 9	Motorway & junction	⊖	Underground station
Services	Motorway service area	⊖	Light railway & station
	Primary road single/dual carriageway	+++++++++++	Preserved private railway
Services	Primary road service area	LC	Level crossing
	A road single/dual carriageway	•—•—•—•—•	Tramway
	B road single/dual carriageway	- - - - - - - -	Ferry route
	Other road single/dual carriageway	....	Airport runway
	Minor/private road, access may be restricted	- · - · - · -	County, administrative boundary
← ←	One-way street	▼▼▼▼▼▼▼▼▼	Mounds
	Pedestrian area	17	Page continuation 1:15,000
=============	Track or footpath	3	Page continuation to enlarged scale 1:10,000
▬▬▬▬▬▬▬	Road under construction		River/canal, lake, pier
⌐ = = = ⌐	Road tunnel		Aqueduct, lock, weir
AA	AA Service Centre	465 ▲ Winter Hill	Peak (with height in metres)
P	Parking		Beach
P+🚌	Park & Ride		Woodland
🚌	Bus/coach station		Park
⇌	Railway & main railway station	† † † †	Cemetery
⇌	Railway & minor railway station		Built-up area

Featured building

City wall

A&E Hospital with 24-hour A&E department

PO Post Office

Public library

i Tourist Information Centre

Petrol station
Major suppliers only

† Church/chapel

Public toilets

Toilet with disabled facilities

PH Public house
AA recommended

Restaurant
AA inspected

Theatre or performing arts centre

Cinema

Golf course

Camping
AA inspected

Caravan Site
AA inspected

Camping & caravan site
AA inspected

Theme park

Abbey, cathedral or priory

Castle

Historic house or building

Wakehurst Place NT National Trust property

Museum or art gallery

Roman antiquity

Ancient site, battlefield or monument

Industrial interest

Garden

Arboretum

Farm or animal centre

Zoological or wildlife collection

Bird collection

Nature reserve

Visitor or heritage centre

Country park

Cave

Windmill

Distillery, brewery or vineyard

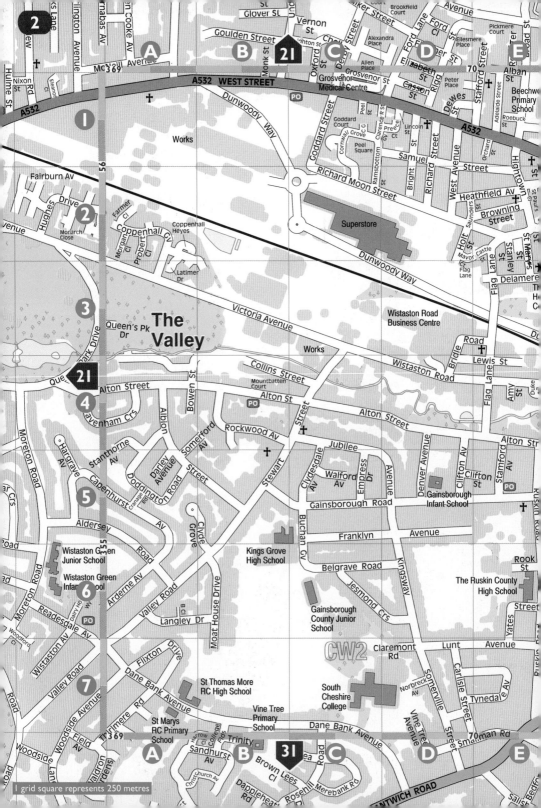

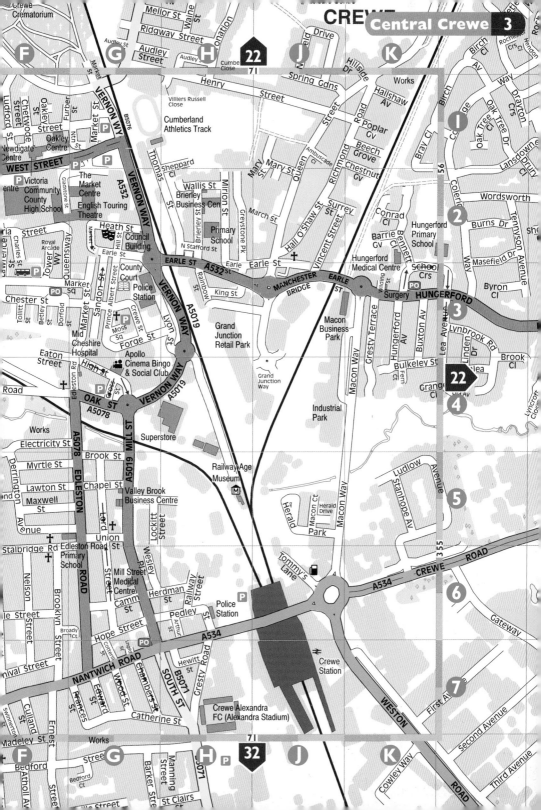

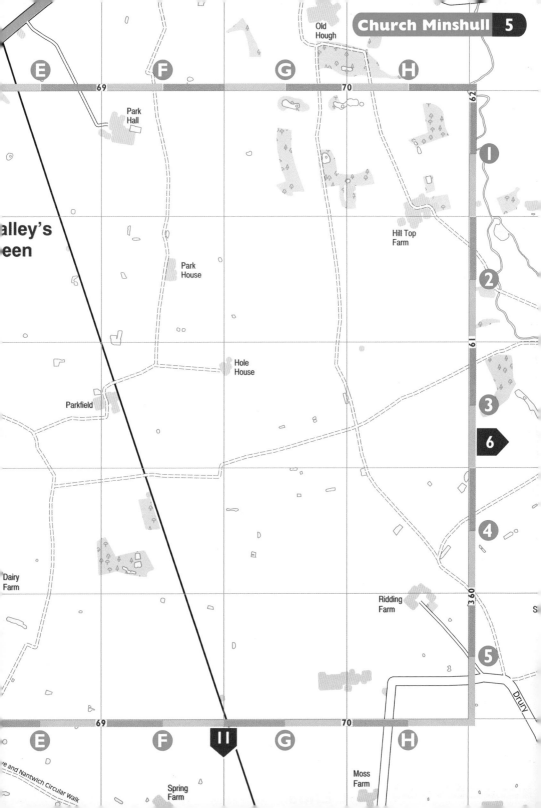

Old Hough

E   F   G   H

69   70   62

Park Hall

alley's
een

Park House

Hill Top Farm

I

2

Hole House

61

3

Parkfield

6

4

Dairy Farm

Ridding Farm

360

5

E   F   **II**   G   H

69   70   Drury

ve and Nantwich Circular Walk

Spring Farm

Moss Farm

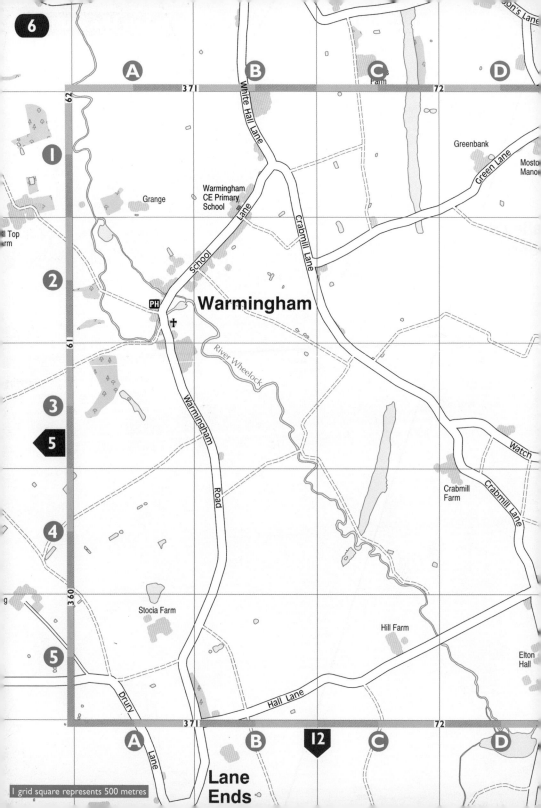

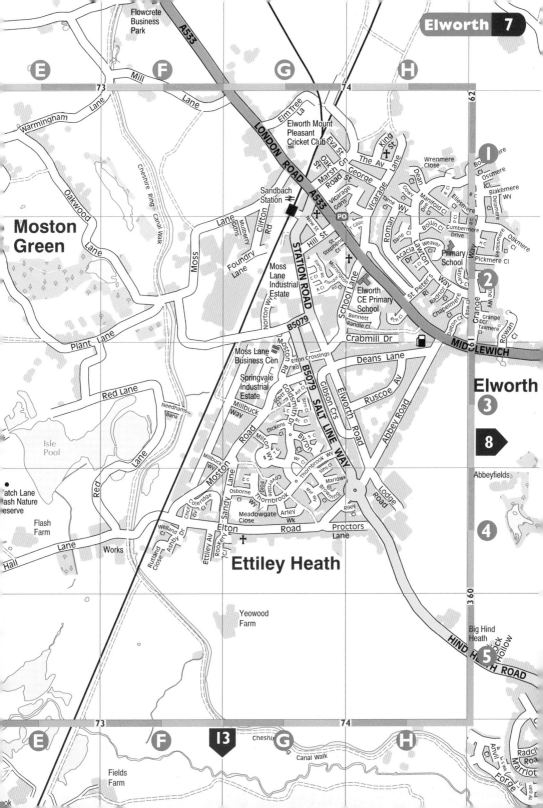

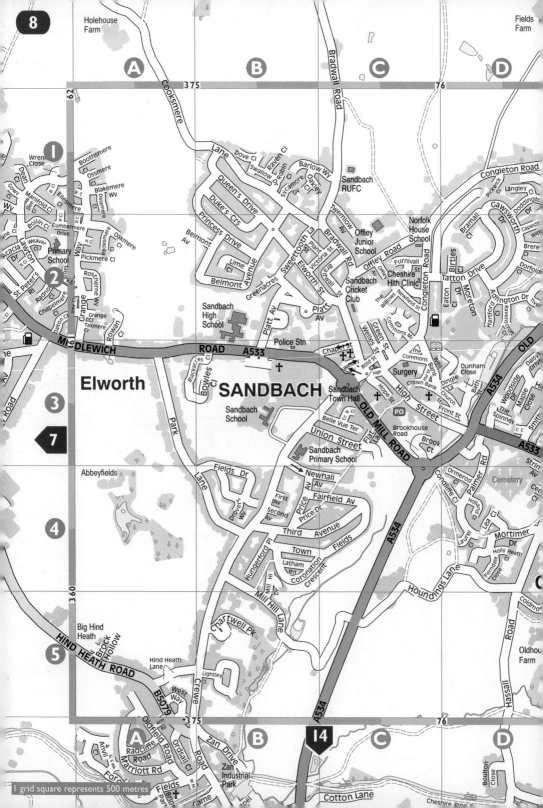

E   F   G   H

Brickhouses

HOLMES CHAPEL RO

77   78   A6234

Junction 17

CONGLETON ROAD

Hotel

Park House

Arclid Industrial Estate

Arclid C

I

ROAD

Oak Farm

Reynold's Farm

Arclid Cottage Farm

Hemmings

Sandbach Heath

/11

Church Lane

M6

William Drive

Oakwood Crs

Skeath Close

Wright's Lane

PO

Heath

Bailey Crs

Peartree Cl

St Johns CE Primary School

Reynold's Lane

61

Heath Road

School Lane

St John's Way

Manor Road

Brookland Dr

Manor

The Hill

HILL

Reynold's Lane

2

3

Betchton Heath

The Cross

Moss Heath

Colley Lane

Boults Green Farm

Sandbach Service Area

Stannerhouse Lane

4

5

360

Pear Tree Farm

Manor House

A533 NEWCASTLE

E   F   G   H

77   78

15

Dean Hill

ROAD

alkin's nk

Brook Farm

Woody Fields

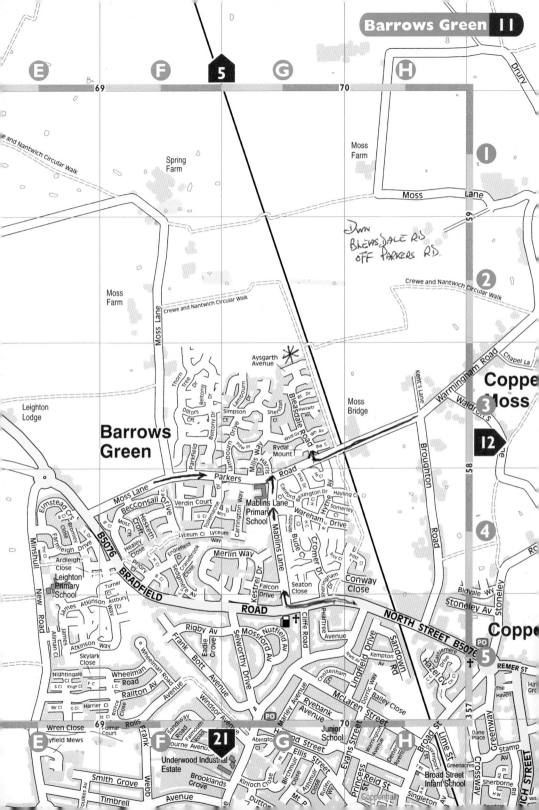

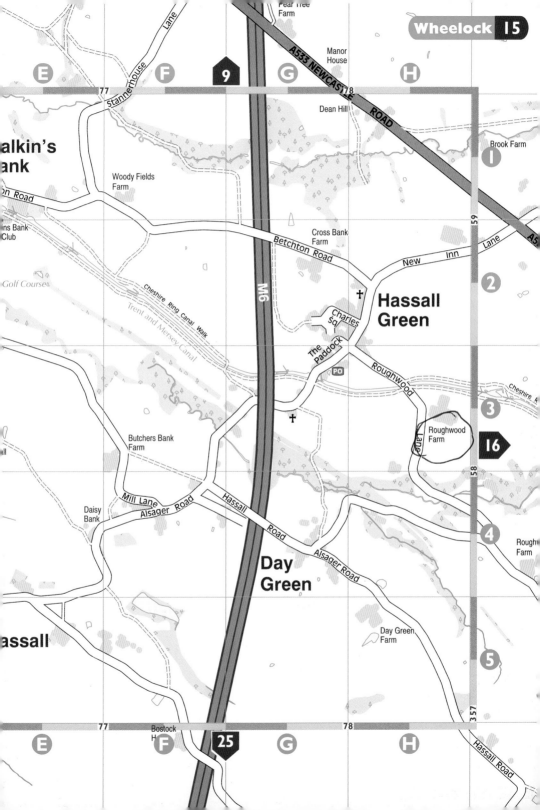

16

A   B   C   Fourlan End   D

CASTLE RD

Love Lane Farm

Love Lane

NEWCASTLE ROAD A50

PH   80

1   Brook Farm   Be Fa

New   Inn   Lane   Love Lane   Betchton House   Lynnhou Farm

A533

2   CAPPERS LANE   Love   Lane

ssall
een

59

3   Cheshire Ring Canal Walk   SANDBACH ROAD A533   South Cheshire way

Roughwood F   Chellshill

15

58

4   Roughwood Hill Farm   B5078   Cheshire Ring Canal Walk   **Thurlwo**

Sandbach Rd   spring Close

shelley Close   Keats D   Tennyson Ct

Lane   Low   Street   Farms Rd

5   Betchton Farm

een

3 57

A   B   **26** Lawton Heath End   C   D

Hassall Road   Dunwood   Denford Pl   Cherry   Lane

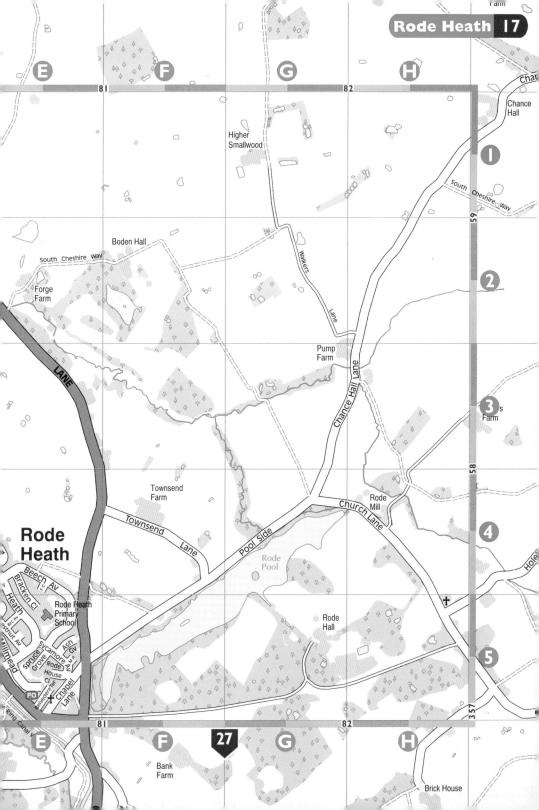

E 81 F 82 G H

Farm

Chance Hall

Chat

1

South Cheshire Way

Higher Smallwood

2

59

Boden Hall

Walkers Lane

South Cheshire Way

Forge Farm

Pump Farm

3

s Farm

LANE

Chance Hall Lane

58

Townsend Farm

Rode Mill

Rode Church Lane

4

Rode Heath

Townsend Lane

Pool Side

Rode Pool

Hole

Beech Av

Bracken Cl

Heath

Rode Heath Primary School

Rode Hall

†

Brc Av

nut Av

Spruce Av

Sycamore Grove

Ash Gv

Rode

House

Cl

5

Millmead

Belvedere Ter

PO

Chapel Lane

57

Ring Canal V

81 82

E F **27** G H

Bank Farm

Brick House

18

Crossbanks Farm

Stokehall Lane

A 363 **B** **C** 64 **D**

57

1

Stoke Hall

Lower Hall

Gates Farm

56

2

Dairy Lane

3

Wettenhall Road

Poole Old Hall Lane

Poole Bank Farm

355

Hurleston Junction

4

Poole House Farm

5

New Farm

Poolehill

Rease Heath

Crewe and Nantwich Circular Walk

Cinder Lane

A51(T)

A 363 **B** **28** **C** 64 **D**

Wetten

Henhullbridge Farm

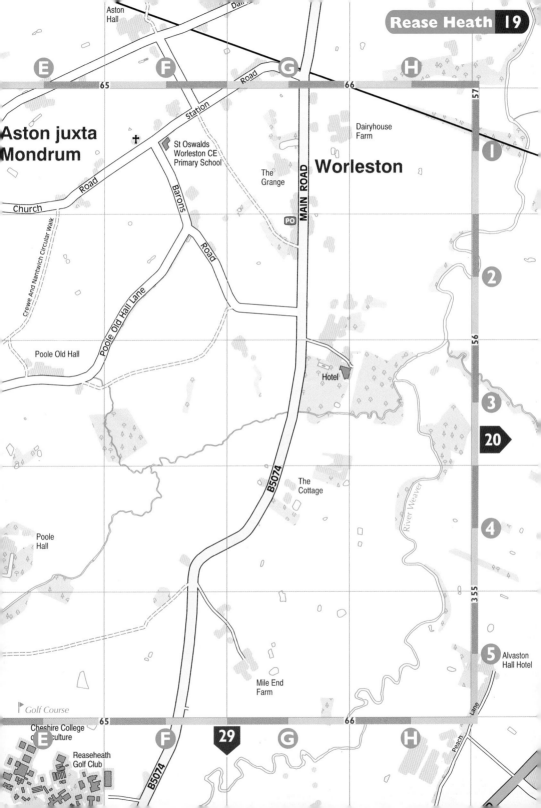

Aston Hall

E 65 F Station G 66 57 H

Aston juxta Mondrum

St Oswalds Worleston CE Primary School

The Grange

MAIN ROAD

Worleston

Dairyhouse Farm

I

Church Road

Barons Road

PO

Crewe And Nantwich Circular Walk

Poole Old Hall Lane

Poole Old Hall

56

Hotel

3

20

B5074

The Cottage

River Weaver

2

4

Poole Hall

3 55

5 Alvaston Hall Hotel

Golf Course

Mile End Farm

Cheshire College of Agriculture

E 65 F 29 G 66 H

Reaseheath Golf Club

B5074

Peach Lane

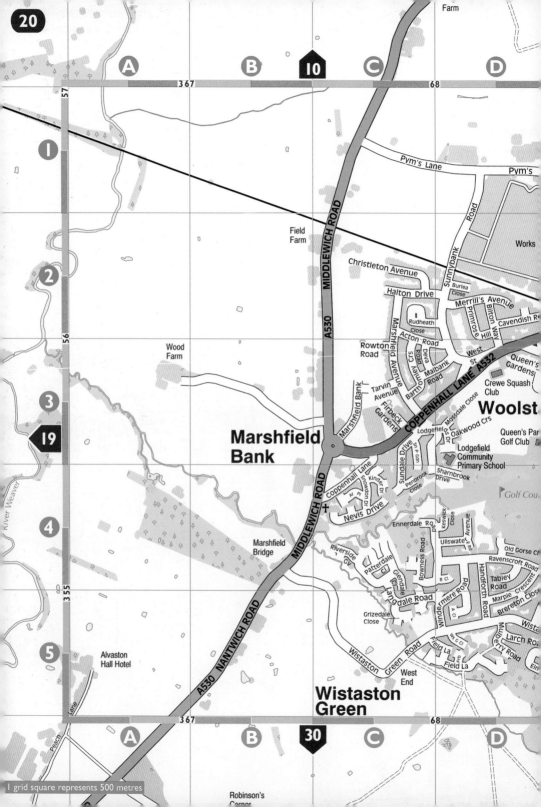

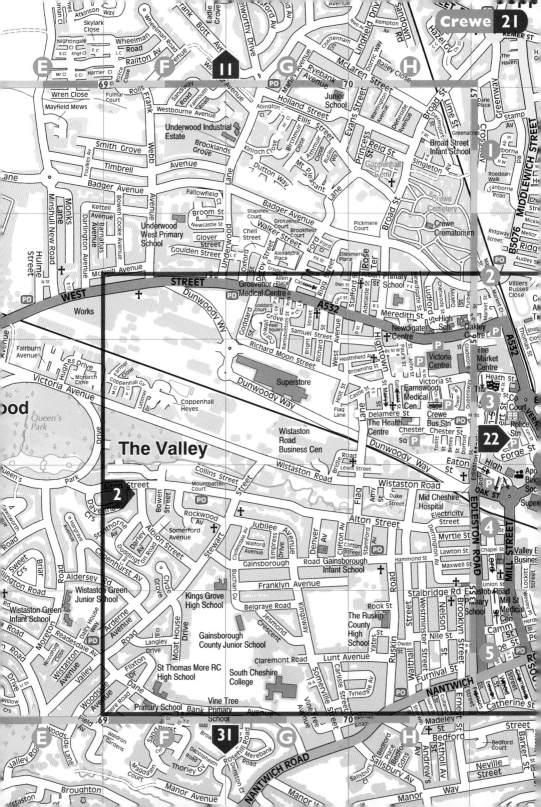

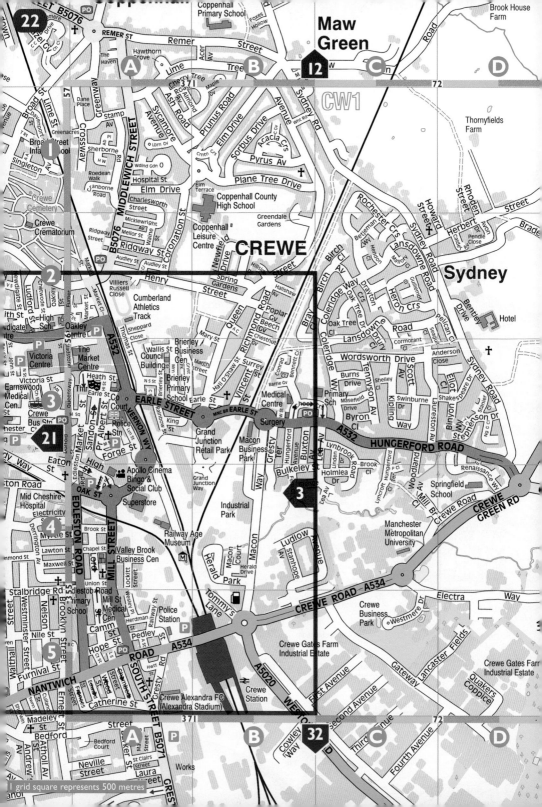

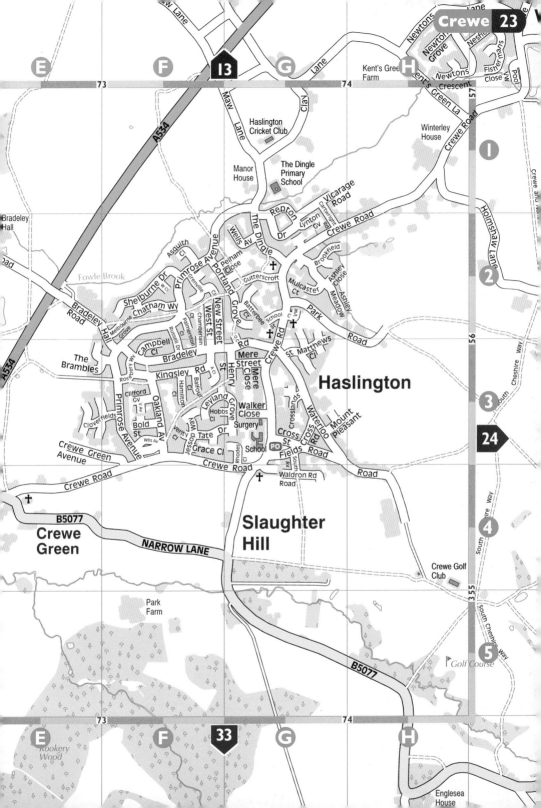

Farm

E
F
15
G
H

77
78
57

Bostock
House

Hassall Road

Heath
End

I

Green Bank
Farm

Pikemere
Primary
School

Hassall Road

Dunnocks Fold
Farm

2

M6

Manor
Farm

Heath
Drive

56

Manchester
Metropolitan
University

3

Windsor
Drive

Dunnocksfold

Road

Sunnyside

spencer
Cl

Lindsay
Wy

Cl

26

Cl

Delamere
Court

Derwent Cl

Dart Cl

Hellyar

Brook

Cranberry
Primary
School

Rye Cl

Arrowsmith Dr

The
Conifers

Bolin

Woodd

Cranfield
Dr

Cranford
Mews

Padston Dr

Sinclair
Av

CLIVE RD

Moss
Farm

Kensington
Court

Nursery Road

Valley Cl

whic

wvr Cl

M La
M Cl
Cr Ms La

Cranberry Lane

4

Lane

Dane
Cl

Moss
Fields

Moss
Way

ALSAG

Gowy Cl

M Cl

Coronation Avenue

The
Close

355

Oakhanger
Moss

Plough
Croft

Close La

5

White
Moss

E
F
35
G
H

77
78

akh..ger
B507
B5078

Works

BUTTERTON LANE
ROAD
LC

Radway

Business &

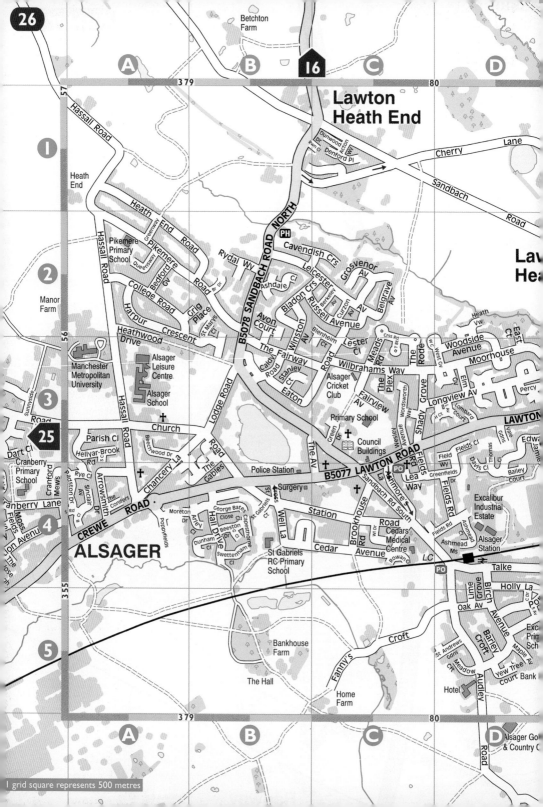

Millmead

Ash GV
Spruce
Sycamore
Grove
Rode
House
Cl

Chapel Lane

E

F

17

G

H

81

82

57

re Ring Canal Wk

Bank Farm

Brick House

I

n Heath Road
ands t

KNUTSFORD ROAD A50

Knutsford Road

Ashbank Farm

2

Church Lawton Gate CP School

Cherry Tree AV

Meadow Wy

Barwood AV

Greengate Rd

Brattswood Drive

Woodgate AV

Brown AV

Grove AV

Church Lawton Primary School

Trent & Mersey Canal

Cheshire Ring Canal Wk

56

Church Lawton

The Grove

Liverpool Road West

Grove Park AV

Elmwood Cl

Crossways Road

LIVERPOOL

ROAD

3

Lawton Hall

Lawton-gate

CREWE ROAD

Dairylands Road

WEST

AV

LINLEY LANE A5011

Cheshire Ring Canal Wk

LC

4

Clowes Avenue
Cl

Linley Grove
Ashenhurst
Nelson Grove

Barratt Rd

Hazel Gv

Foden AV

Linley

355

Elsby Rd

aig Walk

Wayside

Linley

Road

KIDSGROVE

5

Old Butt Lane
Chapel St
Glebe Cl
Skellern St
Wright

Church St
Towr

TON ROAD

Bant
Mi

81

82

E

F

G

H

Nelson Industrial Estate

▶ *Golf Course*

LINLEY

Linley Hall

est

Linley
Tr

Butt Lane

St Saviours

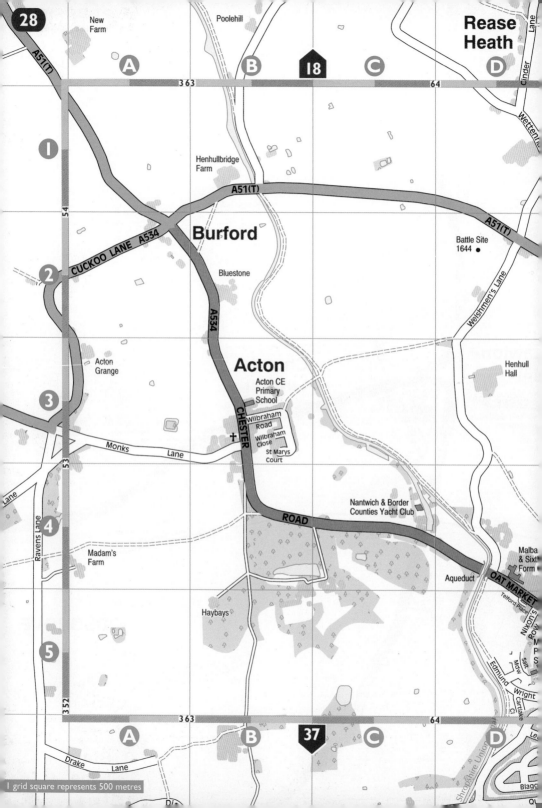

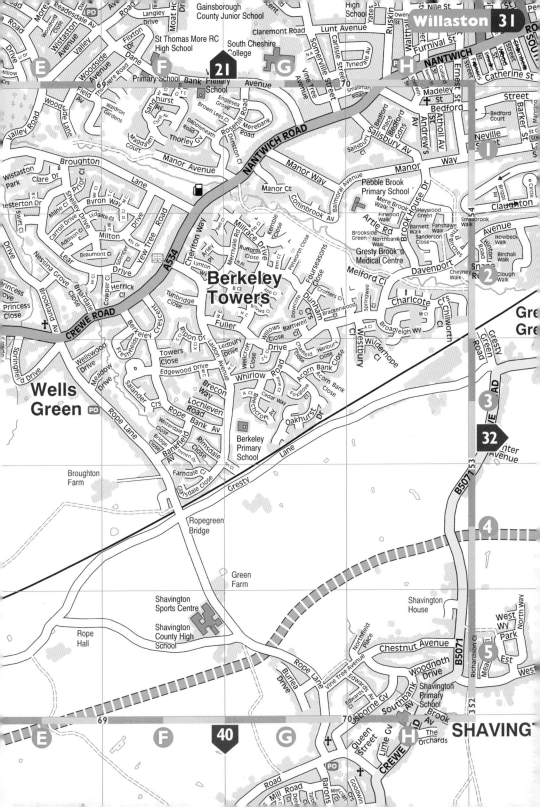

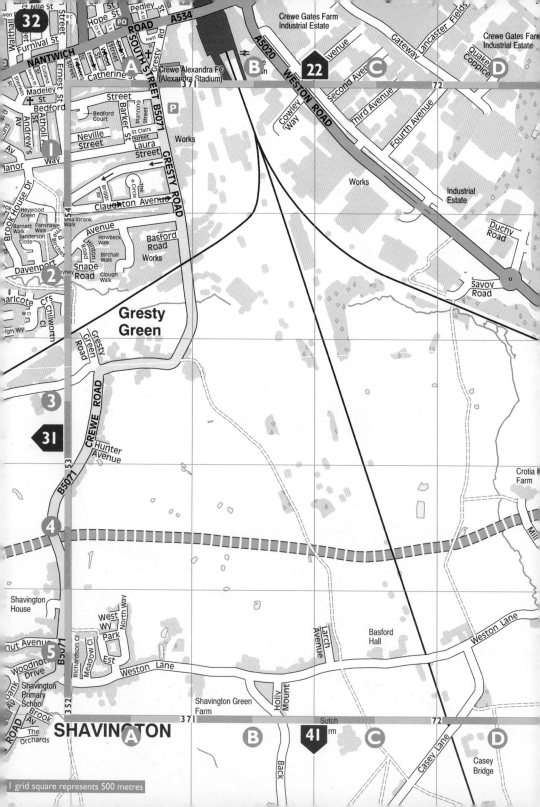

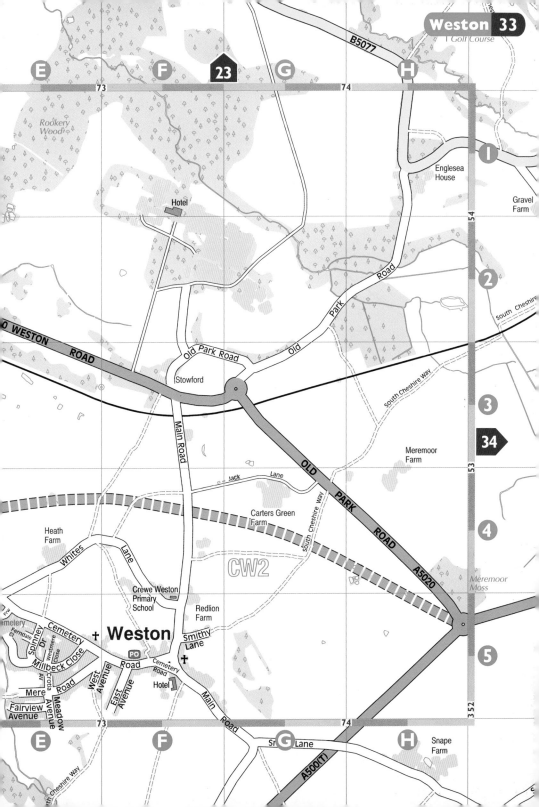

Golf Course

E F 23 G H

73 74

Rookery Wood

Englesea House

Gravel Farm

Hotel

I

54

2

B5077

South Cheshire

WESTON ROAD

Old Park Road

Old Park Road

South Cheshire Way

3

34

Stowford

Meremoor Farm

53

Main Road

Jack Lane

Lane

OLD PARK ROAD A5020

4

Heath Farm

Carters Green Farm

South Cheshire Way

Meremoor Moss

Whites Lane

CW2

Crewe Weston Primary School

Redlion Farm

Cemetery

Spinney Dr

Ferndale Ct

Westmere Close

Weston

Smithy Lane

Millbeck Close

Crota Road

Cemetery Road

5

Mere

Fairview Avenue

West Avenue

East Avenue

Meadow Avenue

PO

Road

Hotel

Main Road

3 52

73 74

E F Sn Lane G H

Snape Farm

South Cheshire Way

A500(T)

34

Golf Course

A

B

24   B5077

C

D

Holmshaw Lane

Butter

375

76

BUTTERTON LANE

Englesea
House

I

Valley Brook

Mill Lane

†

54

Gravel
Farm

Barthomley Road

LC

2

South Cheshire Way

Bridgehouse
Farm

Mill Lane

Mill
Farm

Cheshire Way

3

Smith's
Green

Mill Lane

Dais
Farm

33

Meremoor
Farm

53

Monneley
Farm

Barthomley Road

Barthomley Road

A500(T)

4

A5020

A500(T)

Barthomley

Smithy
Lane

Road

5

Meremoor
Moss

Town House
Farm

Dean's Lane

352

375

76

A

B

C

D

Snape
Farm

ape Lane

I grid square represents 500 metres

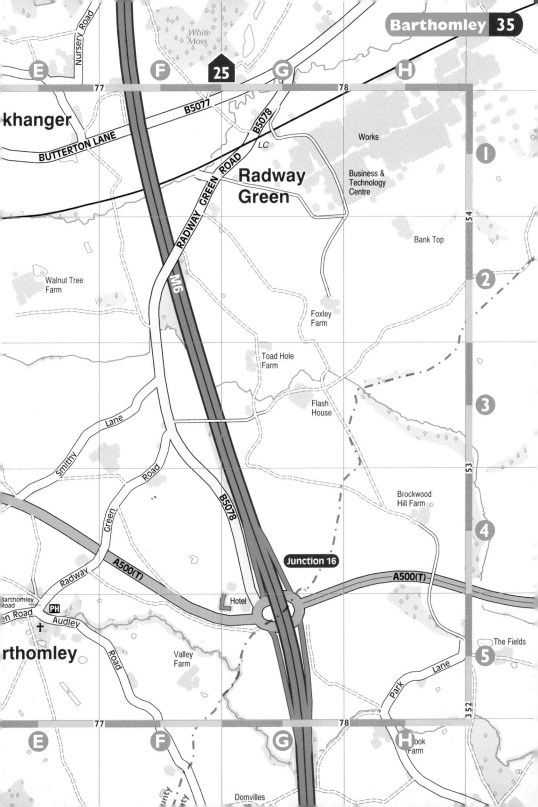

E F **25** G H

77 B5077 78

I

khanger

BUTTERTON LANE

B5078

LC

Works

Radway Green

Business & Technology Centre

54

Bank Top

2

Walnut Tree Farm

M6

Foxley Farm

Toad Hole Farm

3

Flash House

53

Lane

Smithy

Road

Green

Brockwood Hill Farm

4

B5078

A500(T)

Junction 16

A500(T)

Radway

Barthomley Road

en Road

PH

† Audley

Hotel

The Fields

5

rthomley

Road

Valley Farm

Park Lane

352

77 78

E F G H ook Farm

Domvilles

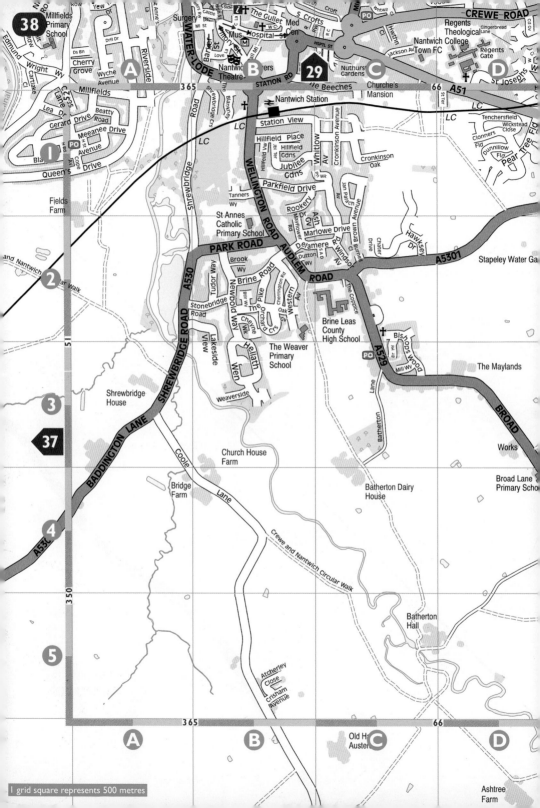

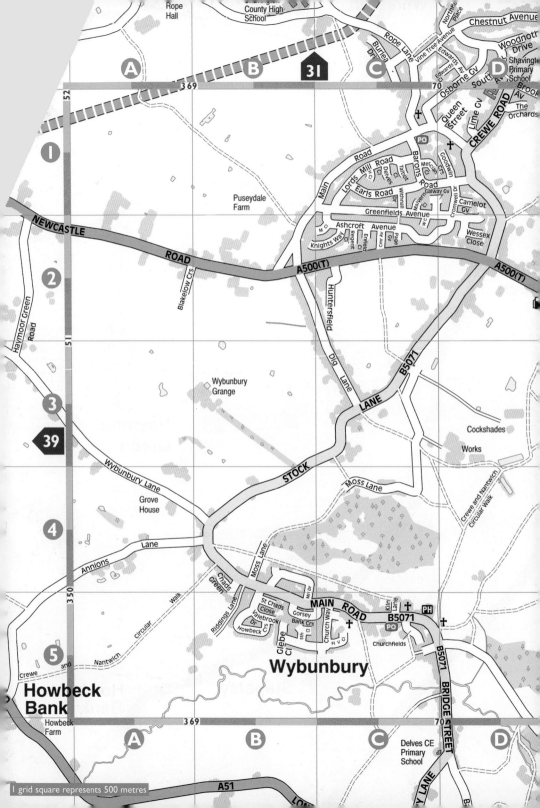

Rope Hall

Shavington County High School

A **B** 31 **C** 70 **D**

Chestnut Avenue

Woodnoth Drive

Shavington Primary School

The Orchards

Rope Lane

Burlea Dr

Vine Tree Avenue

Edwards Av

Osborne Gv

Queen Street

Lime Gv

South

Brook Av

CREWE ROAD

1

52

3 6 9

Puseydale Farm

Main Road

Lords Mill Road

Delves

Talbot

Barons Road

Mercer

Goodwin

PO

Earls Road

Withhall

Calway Gv

Cromwell Dr

Camelot Gv

Wessex Close

Greenfields Avenue

Ashcroft Avenue

Knights Way

Regent

Enfield

Page Gv

Av Gv

NEWCASTLE

ROAD

A500(T)

A500(T)

2

51

Blakelow Crs

Huntersfield

B5071

Haymoor Green Road

Wybunbury Grange

Dig Lane

3

39

Wybunbury Lane

LANE

Cockshades

Works

STOCK

Grove House

Moss Lane

Crewe and Nantwich Circular Walk

4

Lane

Annions

350

Moss Lane

Chads Green

Riddings Lane

Circular Walk

Mrr Dr

St Chads Close

Valebrook Dr

Gorsey Bank Crs

Howbeck

Glebe Cl

Church Way

MAIN ROAD

Kiln Lane

PH

B5071

PO

Churchfields

5

Crewe and Nantwich

Howbeck Bank

Wybunbury

B5071

BRIDGE STREET

Howbeck Farm

3 6 9

70

A **B** **C** **D**

Delves CE Primary School

A51

LONG

I grid square represents 500 metres

Acton	28 B3	Coppenhall Moss	12 A3	Lawton Heath End	26 C1	Stoneley Green	36
Alsager	26 A4	Crewe	22 B2	Malkin's Bank	15 E1	Sydney	22
Aston juxta Mondrum	19 E1	Crewe Green	23 E4	Marshfield Bank	20 B3	Thurlwood	16
The Barony	29 G4	Cross Lane	4 C3	Maw Green	12 C5	Walley's Green	5
Barrows Green	11 E3	Day Green	15 G4	Moston Green	7 E2	Warmingham	6
Barthomley	35 E5	Elworth	8 A3	Nantwich	29 G4	Wells Green	31
Berkeley Towers	31 F2	Ettiley Heath	7 G4	Oakhanger	35 E1	Weston	33
Betchton Heath	9 F4	Gresty Green	32 A2	Radway Green	35 G1	Wheelock	14
Blakelow	39 G1	Haslington	23 G3	Ravensmoor	36 C3	Wheelock Heath	14
Bradfield Green	10 D1	Hassall	15 E5	Rease Heath	18 D5	Willaston	30
Brickhouses	9 F1	Hassall Green	15 H2	Rode Heath	17 E4	Winterley	14
Burford	28 B2	Haymoor Green	39 H3	Sandbach	8 B3	Wistaston	30
Butt Green	39 E2	Hough	41 G3	Sandbach Heath	9 E3	Wistaston Green	20
Chorlton	41 H4	Howbeck Bank	39 H5	Shavington	40 D1	Woolstanwood	20
Church Lawton	27 G3	Kidsgrove	27 H5	Slaughter Hill	23 G4	Worleston	19
Church Minshull	4 A4	Lane Ends	12 B1	Smith's Green	34 D3	Wybunbury	40
Cold Moss Heath	8 D4	Lawton-gate	27 E3	Snow Hill	29 E4		
Coppenhall	12 A5	Lawton Heath	26 D2	Stapeley	39 G5		

USING THE STREET INDEX

Street names are listed alphabetically. Each street name is followed by its postal town or area locality, the Postcode District, the page number, and the reference to the square in which the name is found.

Standard index entries are shown as follows:

Abbey Flds *CW/SHV* CW2 ......**30** C2

Street names and selected addresses not shown on the map due to scale restrictions are shown in the index with an asterisk:

Badgers Wd *CW/SHV* * CW2......**30** D2

GENERAL ABBREVIATIONS

ACC	ACCESS	E	EAST	LDG	LODGE	R	RIVE
ALY	ALLEY	EMB	EMBANKMENT	LGT	LIGHT	RBT	ROUNDABO
AP	APPROACH	EMBY	EMBASSY	LK	LOCK	RD	RO/
AR	ARCADE	ESP	ESPLANADE	LKS	LAKES	RDG	RID
ASS	ASSOCIATION	EST	ESTATE	LNDG	LANDING	REP	REPUBL
AV	AVENUE	EX	EXCHANGE	LTL	LITTLE	RES	RESERVO
BCH	BEACH	EXPY	EXPRESSWAY	LWR	LOWER	RFC	RUGBY FOOTBALL CLU
BLDS	BUILDINGS	EXT	EXTENSION	MAG	MAGISTRATE	RI	RI
BND	BEND	F/O	FLYOVER	MAN	MANSIONS	RP	RAN
BNK	BANK	FC	FOOTBALL CLUB	MD	MEAD	RW	RO
BR	BRIDGE	FK	FORK	MDW	MEADOWS	S	SOU
BRK	BROOK	FLD	FIELD	MEM	MEMORIAL	SCH	SCHO
BTM	BOTTOM	FLDS	FIELDS	MKT	MARKET	SE	SOUTH EA
BUS	BUSINESS	FLS	FALLS	MKTS	MARKETS	SER	SERVICE ARI
BVD	BOULEVARD	FLS	FLATS	ML	MALL	SH	SHO
BY	BYPASS	FM	FARM	ML	MILL	SHOP	SHOPPI
CATH	CATHEDRAL	FT	FORT	MNR	MANOR	SKWY	SKYW
CEM	CEMETERY	FWY	FREEWAY	MS	MEWS	SMT	SUMM
CEN	CENTRE	FY	FERRY	MSN	MISSION	SOC	SOCIE
CFT	CROFT	GA	GATE	MT	MOUNT	SP	SP
CH	CHURCH	GAL	GALLERY	MTN	MOUNTAIN	SPR	SPRIN
CHA	CHASE	GDN	GARDEN	MTS	MOUNTAINS	SQ	SQUA
CHYD	CHURCHYARD	GDNS	GARDENS	MUS	MUSEUM	ST	STRE
CIR	CIRCLE	GLD	GLADE	MWY	MOTORWAY	STN	STATIC
CIRC	CIRCUS	GLN	GLEN	N	NORTH	STR	STRE/
CL	CLOSE	GN	GREEN	NE	NORTH EAST	STRD	STRAN
CLFS	CLIFFS	GND	GROUND	NW	NORTH WEST	SW	SOUTH WE
CMP	CAMP	GRA	GRANGE	O/P	OVERPASS	TDG	TRADI
CNR	CORNER	GRG	GARAGE	OFF	OFFICE	TER	TERRA
CO	COUNTY	GT	GREAT	ORCH	ORCHARD	THWY	THROUGHW
COLL	COLLEGE	GTWY	GATEWAY	OV	OVAL	TNL	TUNN
COM	COMMON	GV	GROVE	PAL	PALACE	TOLL	TOLLW
COMM	COMMISSION	HGR	HIGHER	PAS	PASSAGE	TPK	TURNPI
CON	CONVENT	HL	HILL	PAV	PAVILION	TR	TRA
COT	COTTAGE	HLS	HILLS	PDE	PARADE	TRL	TRA
COTS	COTTAGES	HO	HOUSE	PH	PUBLIC HOUSE	TWR	TOW
CP	CAPE	HOL	HOLLOW	PK	PARK	U/P	UNDERPA
CPS	COPSE	HOSP	HOSPITAL	PKWY	PARKWAY	UNI	UNIVERSI
CR	CREEK	HRB	HARBOUR	PL	PLACE	UPR	UPP
CREM	CREMATORIUM	HTH	HEATH	PLN	PLAIN	V	VA
CRS	CRESCENT	HTS	HEIGHTS	PLNS	PLAINS	VA	VALL
CSWY	CAUSEWAY	HVN	HAVEN	PLZ	PLAZA	VIAD	VIADU
CT	COURT	HWY	HIGHWAY	POL	POLICE STATION	VIL	VIL
CTRL	CENTRAL	IMP	IMPERIAL	PR	PRINCE	VIS	VIS
CTS	COURTS	IN	INLET	PREC	PRECINCT	VLG	VILLA
CTYD	COURTYARD	IND EST	INDUSTRIAL ESTATE	PREP	PREPARATORY	VLS	VILL
CUTT	CUTTINGS	INF	INFIRMARY	PRIM	PRIMARY	VW	VIE
CV	COVE	INFO	INFORMATION	PROM	PROMENADE	W	WE
CYN	CANYON	INT	INTERCHANGE	PRS	PRINCESS	WD	WOO
DEPT	DEPARTMENT	IS	ISLAND	PRT	PORT	WHF	WHA
DL	DALE	JCT	JUNCTION	PT	POINT	WK	WA
DM	DAM	JTY	JETTY	PTH	PATH	WKS	WAL
DR	DRIVE	KG	KING	PZ	PIAZZA	WLS	WEL
DRO	DROVE	KNL	KNOLL	QD	QUADRANT	WY	W
DRY	DRIVEWAY	L	LAKE	QU	QUEEN	YD	YA
DWGS	DWELLINGS	LA	LANE	QY	QUAY	YHA	YOUTH HOST

OSTCODE TOWNS AND AREA ABBREVIATIONS

'/KID ....Alsager/Kidsgrove
G...Congleton
CW/HAS.............Crewe/Haslington
CW/SHV................Crewe/Shavington
MWCH.........................Middlewich
NANT..............................Nantwich
SBCH..........................Sandbach

Index - streets

Abb - Cha

A

ey Flds CW/SHV CW2 ....30 C2
ey Pl CW/HAS CW1 ....22 A1
ey Rd SBCH CW11 ....7 H3
ootsbury Cl CW/SHV CW2 ....31 G2
ngton Cl CW/HAS CW1 ....21 C1
icia Crs CW/HAS CW1 ....22 B1
ord Cl SBCH CW11 ....7 H2
r Av CW/HAS CW1 ....12 B5
rn Bank Cl CW/SHV CW2 ....31 G3
on Rd CW/SHV CW2 ....20 C2
on Wy ALS/KID ST7 ....26 C1
ison Cl CW/SHV CW2 ....31 E2
laide St CW/HAS CW1 ....2 E1
ngton Dr SBCH CW11 ....8 D2
ngton Rd CW/SHV CW2 ....21 E4
ur St CW/HAS CW1 ....2 E1
ert St CW/HAS CW1 ....3 F1
NANT CW5 ....29 F4
on St CW/SHV CW2 ....2 A4
erley Cl CW/HAS CW1 ....9 E2
ersey Rd CW/SHV CW2 ....21 E4
ord Cl CW/SHV CW2 ....41 F3
xandra Pl CW/HAS CW1 ....21 G2
han Cl CW/HAS CW1 ....11 E5
a Av CW/HAS CW1 ....21 H1
ond Av CW/HAS CW1 ....22 A1
BCH CW11 ....15 G4
aston Rd NANT CW5.....................29 G5
aston Wk CW/SHV CW2 ....20 D5
oleside Cl CW/SHV CW2 ....20 D5
ouscade Cl CW/HAS CW1 ....3 J1
y St CW/SHV CW2 ....2 E4
erson Cl CW/HAS CW1 ....22 C3
elina Cl CW/SHV CW2 ....7 G2
ions La NANT CW5 ....40 A4
iil Cl SBCH CW11 ....14 A1
erne Av CW/HAS CW1 ....2 A4
eigh Cl CW/HAS CW1 ....11 E4
y Cl ALS/KID ST7 ....26 B4
y Pl CW/SHV CW2 ....31 F2
y Wk SBCH CW11 ....7 G3
ngton Cl CW/SHV CW2 ....31 H2
ittstead Rd SBCH CW11 ....14 A1
old St NANT CW5 ....29 F4
en Pl CW/SHV CW2 ....20 C4
wsmith Dr ALS/KID ST7...............26 A4
ur St CW/SHV CW2 ....3 H6
e Rd CW/SHV CW2 ....31 H2
ndel Cl CW/HAS CW1 ....30 D2
oy Dr SBCH CW11 ....7 F4
croft Av CW/SHV CW2 ....40 C2
dale Cl ALS/KID ST7 ....26 B2
enhurst Rd ALS/KID ST7 ....27 E4
Gv ALS/KID ST7 ....17 E5
ANT CW5 ....38 B1
ea Dr NANT CW5 ....30 D5
ym Cl CW/HAS CW1 ....23 G2
ley Meadow CW/HAS CW1...........23 G2
mead Cl ALS/KID ST7...................26 D4
mead Ms ALS/KID ST7 ....26 D4
more's La ALS/KID ST7 ....26 C4
muir Cl CW/HAS CW1 ....21 G1
Rd CW/HAS CW1 ....22 A1
ville Ct CW/SHV CW2 ....31 G3
dale Cl ALS/KID ST7 ....26 B2
oury Cl CW/HAS CW1 ....23 F2
erley Cl NANT CW5.......................38 B5
oll Av CW/SHV CW2 ....31 H1
vood Cl CW/HAS CW1 ....23 F3
lem Rd NANT CW5 ....38 B2
ley Rd CW/HAS CW1 ....35 E5
ley St CW/HAS CW1 ....22 A2
ten Cl SBCH CW11 ....7 G3
Avenue ALS/KID ST7 ....26 B3
BCH CW11 ....7 H1
n Ct ALS/KID ST7 ....26 B2
n Dr CW/HAS CW1 ....22 D2
garth Av CW/HAS CW1 ....11 G3

B

k La CW/SHV CW2 ....41 F1

Baddiley Cl NANT CW5 ....36 C3
Baddiley La NANT CW5 ....36 A5
Baddington La NANT CW5 ....38 A4
Badger Av CW/HAS CW1 ....21 E1
Badgers Wd CW/SHV * CW2........30 D2
Bagmere Cl SBCH CW11 ....8 A2
Bailey Cl CW/HAS CW1 ....11 H5
Bailey Ct ALS/KID ST7 ....26 D4
Bailey Crs SBCH CW11 ....9 E3
Balfour Cl CW/HAS CW1 ....23 F3
Balmoral Av CW/SHV CW2 ....31 G1
Balmoral Pl NANT CW5 ....39 G1
Bankfield Av CW/SHV CW2 ....31 F3
Bannacks Cl NANT CW5................30 C4
Barker St CW/HAS CW1 ....32 A1
NANT CW5 ....29 F5
Barley Cft ALS/KID ST7 ....26 D5
Barleywood Cl CW/SHV CW2 ....31 G2
Barlow Wy SBCH CW11 ....8 B1
Barnabas Av CW/HAS CW1 ....21 E2
Barnes Cl CW/HAS * CW1 ....23 F3
Barnett Wk CW/SHV CW2 ....31 H2
Barnwell Cl CW/SHV CW2 ....31 G2
Baronia Pl NANT CW5 ....29 F4
Barons Rd CW/SHV CW2 ....40 C1
NANT CW5 ....19 F1
Barony Buildings NANT CW5 ....29 F4
Barony Ct NANT CW5 ....29 F3
Barony Rd NANT CW5 ....29 F3
Barony Ter NANT * CW5 ....29 F4
Barracks La NANT CW5 ....36 D3
Barratt Rd ALS/KID ST7 ....27 E4
Barrie Gv CW/HAS CW1 ....3 K2
Barrows Cl CW/HAS CW1 ....11 F4
Barthomley Crs CW/SHV CW2 .....20 C3
Barthomley Rd CW/HAS CW1 ......34 A1
CW/SHV CW2 ....34 D4
Barwood Av CW/SHV CW2 ....31 H1
Basford Rd CW/SHV CW2 ....32 A2
Batemans Cl CW/SHV CW2 ....31 G2
Atherton La NANT CW5.................38 C3
Bath St SBCH CW11 ....8 D3
Batterbee Ct CW/HAS CW1 ....23 G2
Bayley Rd NANT CW5 ....30 C5
Beam Heath Wy NANT CW5..........29 G3
Beam St NANT CW5 ....29 F5
Beatty Rd NANT CW5 ....38 A1
Beaumont Cl CW/SHV CW2 ....31 E2
Becconsall Cl CW/HAS CW1 ....11 F4
Becconsall Dr CW/HAS CW1 ....11 F4
Beckford Cl CW/HAS CW1.............11 E4
Bedford Ct CW/SHV CW2 ....32 A1
Bedford Gdns CW/SHV CW2 ....31 H1
Bedford Gv ALS/KID ST7 ....26 C2
Bedford Pl CW/SHV CW2 ....31 H1
Bedford St CW/SHV CW2 ....31 H1
Beech Av ALS/KID ST7 ....17 E4
Beechcroft Av CW/SHV CW2 ....31 G3
The Beeches NANT CW5 ....29 F5
Beech Dr CW/SHV CW2 ....20 D5
Beech Gv CW/HAS CW1 ....3 K1
SBCH CW11 ....9 E3
Beech St West CW/HAS * CW1 ....2 E2
Beech Tree Cl NANT CW5 ....30 C5
Beechwood Dr ALS/KID ST7.........26 A3
Beeston Dr ALS/KID ST7 ....26 B4
Belgrave Av ALS/KID ST7 ....26 C2
Belgrave Rd CW/SHV CW2 ....2 C6
Belle Vue Ter SBCH CW11 ....8 A2
Belmont Av SBCH CW11 ....8 A2
Beltony Dr CW/HAS CW1 ....11 F3
Belvedere Ter ALS/KID ST7...........17 E5
Bennett Cl CW/HAS CW1 ....3 K2
Bennett Randle Cl SBCH CW11 ......7 H2
Bentley Dr CW/HAS CW1 ....22 D2
Berkeley Av ALS/KID ST7 ....26 C2
Berkeley Crs CW/SHV CW2 ....31 F2
Betchton Cl SBCH CW11 ....8 D5
Betchton Rd SBCH CW11 ....14 D1
Betjeman Wy CW/HAS CW1 ....22 C2
Betley St CW/HAS CW1 ....3 F3
Bexington Dr CW/HAS CW1 ....11 G4
Bibby St ALS/KID ST7 ....16 D5
Bickley Cl CW/SHV CW2 ....41 F3
Bidvale Wy CW/HAS CW1 ....11 H4
Billington Cl CW/SHV CW2 ....2 A6
Bilton Wy CW/HAS CW1 ....20 D2
Binyon Wy CW/HAS CW1 ....31 D3
Birchall Wk CW/SHV CW2 ....32 A2

The Birches CW/SHV CW2 ....31 H2
Birch Av ALS/KID ST7 ....26 D4
CW/HAS CW1 ....22 C2
Birch Cl CW/HAS CW1 ....22 C2
Birchfield Av ALS/KID ST7 ....17 E5
Birchin Cl NANT CW5 ....29 H4
Birchin La NANT CW5 ....29 H4
Birch La CW/SHV CW2 ....41 G3
Birchmuir Cl CW/HAS CW1 ....21 G1
Birchwood Dr NANT CW5 ....29 G4
Birtles Cl SBCH CW11 ....8 D2
Bishops Wd NANT CW5 ....38 C2
Blackacres Cl SBCH CW11 ....8 A3
Blackthorn Cl CW/SHV CW2 ....31 G2
Bladon Crs ALS/KID ST7 ....26 B2
Blagg Av NANT CW5 ....37 H1
Blake Cl CW/SHV CW2 ....31 E1
Blakelow Crs NANT CW5 ....40 A2
Blakemere Wy SBCH CW11 ....8 A1
The Blankney NANT CW5 ....29 F5
Bleasdale Rd CW/HAS CW1 ....11 G3
Blenheim Cl CW/SHV * CW2 ....30 D2
Blenheim Ct ALS/KID ST7 ....26 B2
Boden Dr NANT CW5 ....39 G1
Bodnant Cl CW/HAS CW1 ....11 F4
Bold St CW/HAS CW1 ....23 F3
SBCH CW11 ....8 C3
Bollands Rw NANT CW5 ....29 F5
Bollin Cl ALS/KID ST7 ....25 G4
SBCH CW11 ....7 H2
Booth Av SBCH CW11 ....9 E3
Boothsmere Cl NANT CW5 ....8 A1
Borrowdale Cl CW/SHV CW2 ....20 D4
Boulton Cl SBCH CW11 ....14 D1
Bowen Cooke Av CW/HAS CW1....21 F1
Bowen St CW/SHV CW2 ....2 A4
Bowers Rw NANT CW5 ....29 E5
Bowkers Cft SBCH CW11 ....14 A4
Bowland Cft CW/HAS CW1 ....11 G3
Bowles Cl SBCH CW11 ....8 B3
Bowling Green Ct NANT * CW5 ....29 F5
Bowness Rd CW/HAS CW1 ....20 C4
Bowyer Av NANT CW5 ....29 F4
Bracken Cl ALS/KID ST7 ....17 E4
Brackenwood Cl CW/SHV CW2 ....31 G2
Bradeley Hall Rd CW/HAS CW1 ...22 D2
Bradeley Rd CW/HAS CW1 ....23 F3
Bradfield Rd CW/HAS CW1 ....11 F4
Bradwall St SBCH CW11 ....8 C2
Braemar Cl CW/SHV * CW2 ....30 D2
Bramall Cl SBCH CW11 ....8 D2
The Brambles CW/HAS CW1..........23 E3
Bramhall Rd CW/HAS CW1 ....21 E5
Brassey Wy NANT CW5 ....30 C5
Brattswood Dr ALS/KID ST7 ....27 E2
Bray Cl CW/HAS CW1 ....3 K1
Brecon Wy CW/SHV CW2 ....3 H2
Brereton Cl CW/SHV CW2 ....20 D5
SBCH CW11 ....8 D2
Brereton Dr NANT CW5 ....29 G3
Briardale Cl CW/SHV CW2 ....31 G2
Bridge Cl CW/SHV CW2 ....31 F3
Bridgemere Cl SBCH CW11.............8 A1
Bridge St NANT CW5 ....40 D5
Bridle Hey NANT CW5 ....38 C3
Bridle Rd CW/SHV CW2 ....2 D4
Brierley St CW/HAS CW1 ....3 H2
Briggs Av CW/SHV CW2 ....32 A1
Bright St CW/HAS CW1 ....2 D2
Brindley Pk SBCH CW11 ....14 A1
Brine Rd NANT CW5 ....38 B2
Broad La NANT CW5 ....38 D3
Broadleigh Wy CW/SHV CW2 ....31 H2
Broad St CW/HAS CW1 ....21 H2
The Broadway NANT CW5 ....29 G5
Broady Cl CW/SHV CW2 ....3 F6
Brock Hollow SBCH CW11 ....8 A5
Bromley Cl CW/HAS CW1 ....11 E4
Brook Av CW/SHV CW2 ....31 H5
Brook Cl CW/HAS CW1 ....22 C4
Brook St SBCH CW11 ....8 C3
Brookfield CW/HAS CW1 ....23 G2
Brookfield Ct CW/HAS CW1 ....21 G2
Brookfield Dr ALS/KID ST7 ....26 B2
Brook House Dr CW/SHV CW2......31 H2
Brookhouse La CW/HAS CW1 ....4 C3
Brookhouse Rd ALS/KID ST7 ....26 C4
SBCH CW11 ....8 C3
Brookland Av CW/SHV CW2..........31 G2

C

Brookland Dr SBCH CW11 ....9 E3
The Brooklands CW/SHV CW2 ......41 F2
Brooklands Flats CW/HAS * CW1...21 H1
Brooklands Gv CW/HAS CW1 ....21 F1
Brooklyn St CW/SHV CW2 ....3 F6
Brookmere Cl SBCH CW11 ....7 H1
Brookside Gn CW/SHV CW2 ....31 G1
Brook St CW/SHV CW2 ....3 G5
Brook Vls ALS/KID * ST7 ....26 D4
Brook Wy NANT CW5 ....38 B2
Broom St CW/HAS CW1 ....21 F2
Broughton La CW/SHV CW2 ....31 E1
Broughton Rd CW/HAS CW1 ....11 H3
Brown Av ALS/KID ST7 ....27 F3
SBCH CW11 ....38 C2
Browning Cl SBCH CW11 ....7 G4
Browning St CW/HAS CW1 ....2 E2
Brown Lees Cl CW/SHV CW2 ....31 F1
Brunner Gv NANT CW5 ....30 A5
Buchan Gv CW/SHV CW2 ....2 D2
Buckingham Cl CW/SHV CW2 ....30 D2
Buck La CW/SHV CW2 ....41 F2
Bude Cl ALS/KID ST7 ....26 A4
CW/HAS CW1 ....11 G4
Budworth Cl SBCH CW11 ....8 A2
Bulkeley St CW/HAS CW1 ....3 K4
Burjen Wy CW/HAS CW1 ....21 G1
Burlea Cl CW/SHV CW2 ....20 D2
Burlea Dr CW/SHV CW2 ....31 G5
Burnell Ct NANT CW5 ....38 C2
Burns Cl ALS/KID ST7 ....16 D4
Burns Dr CW/HAS CW1 ....22 C3
Burton Gv CW/HAS * CW1 ....11 G3
Butler Wy NANT CW5 ....38 B2
Buttermere Dr CW/HAS CW1 ....11 G3
Butterton La CW/HAS CW1 ....24 C5
CW/HAS CW1 ....34 A1
The Butts ALS/KID ST7 ....26 C3
Buxton Av CW/HAS CW1 ....3 K3
Byron Cl ALS/KID * ST7 ....16 D5
CW/SHV CW2 ....7 G3
SBCH CW11 ....7 G3
Byron Wy CW/SHV CW2 ....31 E1

Caernarvon Rd CW/SHV CW2 ....30 D2
Calder Av CW/HAS CW1 ....22 D2
Caldy Rd ALS/KID ST7 ....26 B3
Camden St CW/HAS * CW1 ....3 H2
Camelot Gv CW/SHV CW2 ....40 D1
Cameron Av CW/SHV CW2 ....40 C2
Camm St CW/SHV CW2 ....3 G6
Campbell Cl CW/HAS CW1 ....23 F3
Canford Cl CW/HAS CW1...............11 G4
Capenhurst Av CW/SHV CW2 ....21 E4
Capesthorne Cl ALS/KID ST7 ....26 B4
SBCH CW11 ....8 D2
Capesthorne Rd CW/SHV CW2......20 D5
Cappers La SBCH CW11 ....16 A2
Carisbrooke Cl CW/SHV CW2 ....30 D2
Carlisle St CW/SHV CW2 ....2 D7
Carlyle Cl ALS/KID ST7 ....16 D4
Carrington Wy CW/HAS CW1 ....11 G4
Carroll Dr CW/SHV CW2 ....31 E2
Cartlake Cl NANT CW5 ....28 D5
Cartwright Rd CW/HAS CW1 ....23 G1
Casey La CW/SHV CW2 ....41 G2
Casson St CW/HAS CW1 ....2 D1
Castlemere Dr CW/HAS CW1 ....11 H5
Castle St CW/HAS CW1 ....2 E2
NANT CW5 ....29 F5
Catherine St CW/SHV CW2 ....3 G7
Cavendish Crs ALS/KID ST7 ....26 B2
Cavendish Rd CW/SHV CW2 ....20 D2
Cecil Rigby Cl SBCH CW11 ....8 C3
Cedar Av ALS/KID ST7 ....26 C4
Cedar Cl SBCH CW11 ....8 D4
Cedar Ct NANT CW5 ....30 C4
Cedar Gv NANT CW5 ....29 H5
Cedar Wy CW/SHV CW2 ....31 G3
Celestria Cl SBCH CW11 ....7 G2
Cemetery Rd CW/SHV CW2 ....33 E5
Chads Gn NANT CW5 ....40 B4
Chalfield Cl CW/SHV CW2 ....31 G3
Chamberlain Ct CW/HAS CW1 ......23 F2
Chambers St CW/SHV CW2 ....3 G7

Chance Hall La *ALS/KID* ST7 ....17 G3
Chancery La *ALS/KID* ST7 ....26 A4
Chantry Ct *CW/HAS* * CW1 ....3 C3
Chapel La *ALS/KID* ST7..........17 E5
CW/HAS CW1 ....12 A3
NANT CW5 ....36 C3
Chapelmere Cl *SBCH* CW11 ....7 H2
Chapelmere Ct *CW/HAS* CW1 ....11 H5
Chapel Rw *NANT* CW5 ....29 E5
Chapel St *CW/SHV* CW2............3 C5
SBCH CW11 ....8 C3
SBCH CW11 ....14 B1
Charlcote Crs *CW/SHV* CW2 ......31 A2
Charles Sq *SBCH* CW11 ....15 C2
Charles St *CW/HAS* CW1 ....3 F2
Charlesworth St *SBCH* CW11......8 D3
Charlesworth St *CW/HAS* CW1 ....22 A1
Chartwell Pk *SBCH* CW11 ....8 B5
Chater Dr *NANT* CW5 ....38 D2
Chatham Wy *CW/HAS* CW1 ....23 F2
Chatsworth Cl *CW/SHV* CW2 ......31 F3
Chaucer Gv *SBCH* CW11 ....7 F4
Cheerbrook Rd *NANT* CW5........39 F1
Chell St *CW/HAS* CW1 ....21 G2
Cheltenham Crs *CW/HAS* CW1....11 C5
Cheriton Wy *CW/HAS* CW1 ......31 F2
Cherrington Rd *NANT* CW5 ......38 B2
Cherry Gv *NANT* CW5............29 E5
Cherry La *ALS/KID* ST7 ....26 D1
Cherry Tree Av *ALS/KID* ST7 ....27 F2
Cherry Tree Rd *CW/HAS* CW1....22 A1
Cheshire Ring Canal Wk
ALS/KID ST7 ....16 C4
SBCH CW11 ....13 G1
Chester Rd *NANT* CW5............28 B3
Chester Sq *CW/HAS* CW1..........2 E3
Chester St *CW/HAS* CW1 ....3 F3
Chesterton Dr *CW/SHV* CW2 ....31 E1
Chesterton Gv *SBCH* CW11........7 G4
Chestnut Av *ALS/KID* ST7 ......17 E5
CW/SHV CW2 ....31 H5
Chestnut Dr *ALS/KID* ST7 ......26 D5
Chestnut Gv *ALS/KID* ST7 ....3 J1
Chetwode St *CW/HAS* CW1 ....3 F1
Cheyne Wk *NANT* CW5 ....38 B2
Cheyney Wk *CW/HAS* CW1 ......31 H2
Chidlow Cl *CW/SHV* CW2..........41 F2
Chilworth Cl *CW/SHV* CW2 ......31 H2
Chorlton La *CW/HAS* CW1 ......41 H4
Christchurch Av *CW/SHV* CW2 ..31 F1
Christleton Av *CW/SHV* CW2 ....20 C2
Churchfields *NANT* CW5 ....40 C5
Church La *ALS/KID* ST7 ....17 G4
CW/SHV CW2 ....30 D3
NANT CW5 ....29 F5
SBCH CW11 ....9 F3
Churchmere Cl *CW/HAS* CW1....11 H5
Church Rd *ALS/KID* ST7 ....26 A3
NANT CW5 ....19 E1
Church St *SBCH* CW11 ....8 C3
Church Vw *CW/HAS* CW1 ....23 G2
Church Wy *NANT* CW5............40 C5
Churchyard Side *NANT* CW5 ....29 F5
Churton Cl *CW/SHV* CW2 ....41 F2
Cinder La *NANT* CW5 ....18 D5
The Circle *CW/SHV* CW2..........32 A1
Circle Av *NANT* CW5..............30 D5
Clare Dr *CW/SHV* CW2 ....31 E1
Claremont Rd *CW/SHV* CW2 ......2 C7
Clarence Gv *CW/HAS* CW1 ....2 C1
Claughton Av *CW/SHV* CW2 ....32 A1
Clay La *CW/HAS* CW1 ....23 C1
SBCH CW11 ....6 D5
Claytons Rw *NANT* CW5 ....29 F3
Cliffe Rd *CW/HAS* CW1 ....11 C5
Clifford Gv *CW/HAS* CW1 ....23 F3
Clifton Av *CW/SHV* CW2 ....2 D5
Clifton Rd *SBCH* CW11............7 G2
Clifton St *CW/SHV* CW2 ....2 D5
Clonners Fld *NANT* CW5 ....38 D1
The Close *ALS/KID* ST7 ....25 H4
Close La *ALS/KID* ST7 ....25 H5
ALS/KID ST7 ....25 G3
Clough Wk *CW/SHV* CW2........32 A1
Cloverfields *CW/HAS* CW1 ......23 E3
Clowes Av *ALS/KID* ST7 ....27 E4
Clyde Gv *CW/HAS* CW1 ....2 B5
Clydesdale Av *CW/SHV* CW2 ......2 C5
Cobbs La *CW/SHV* CW2 ....41 F4
NANT CW5 ....29 F3
Cocoa Yd *NANT* * CW5 ....29 F5
Coldmoss Dr *SBCH* CW11 ....8 D5
Coleridge Cl *SBCH* CW11..........7 F4
Coleridge Wy *CW/HAS* CW1......22 C2
College Flds *CW/SHV* CW2 ......31 F1
College Rd *ALS/KID* ST7 ....26 A2
Colley La *SBCH* CW11............9 E5
Colleys La *NANT* CW5............30 A2

Collinbrook Av *CW/SHV* CW2 ....31 G1
Collins St *CW/SHV* CW2 ....2 B4
Comberbach Dr *NANT* CW5......38 D1
The Commons *SBCH* CW11........8 C5
Commons Ml *SBCH* CW11 ....8 C2
Condliffe Cl *CW/HAS* CW1 ....8 C4
Congleton Rd *SBCH* CW11 ....8 C2
SBCH CW11 ....9 G1
The Conifers *ALS/KID* ST7 ......26 A4
Coniston Cl *NANT* CW5 ....29 H4
Conrad St *CW/HAS* CW1 ....3 K2
Conway St *CW/HAS* CW1 ....11 H4
Coole La *NANT* CW5..............38 A3
Cope Av *NANT* CW5..............38 A1
Copes La *NANT* CW5 ....28 D5
Coppenhall Gv *CW/HAS* CW1 ....2 A2
Coppenhall Heyes *CW/SHV* CW2 ..2 A2
Coppenhall La *NANT* CW5 ......20 C3
The Coppice *NANT* CW5 ....38 C2
SBCH CW11 ....7 H2
Coppice Cl *NANT* CW5 ....30 C4
Coppice Rd *NANT* CW5 ....30 C4
SBCH CW11 ....14 A4
Cormorant Cl *CW/HAS* CW1 ....22 C3
Cornwall Gv *CW/HAS* CW1 ....2 C1
Coronation Av *ALS/KID* ST7 ....25 H4
Coronation Crs *CW/HAS* CW1 ..22 B1
SBCH CW11 ....8 B4
Coronation St *CW/HAS* CW1 ....22 A2
Cotterill St *CW/SHV* CW2 ....3 G7
Cotton La *NANT* CW5 ....14 C1
Coverdale Fold *SBCH* CW11......7 G4
Cowfields *NANT* CW5 ....29 F4
Cowley Wy *CW/HAS* CW1 ......32 B1
Cowper Cl *CW/SHV* CW2 ....31 F2
Crabmill St *SBCH* CW11 ....7 G2
Crabmill La *SBCH* CW11............6 B1
Crabtree Gv *CW/HAS* CW1 ......22 B1
Craig Wk *ALS/KID* ST7 ....27 E5
Cranage Rd *CW/SHV* CW2 ....2 A5
Cranberry La *ALS/KID* ST7 ......25 H4
Cranberry Moss La *ALS/KID* ST7 ...25 H4
Cranborne Av *NANT* CW5 ......22 A1
Cranbrook Cl *CW/HAS* CW1 ....11 F4
Cranfield Dr *ALS/KID* ST7 ......25 H4
Cranford Ms *ALS/KID* ST7 ......25 H4
The Crescent *NANT* CW5........29 G4
Cresswellshawe Rd *ALS/KID* ST7 ...26 C2
Crewe Green Av *CW/HAS* CW1 ..23 E3
Crewe Green Rd *CW/HAS* CW1 ..22 D4
Crewe & Nantwich Cicular Wk
NANT CW5 ....39 F4
CW/HAS CW1 ....4 B3
CW/HAS CW1 ....11 H2
CW/HAS CW1 ....24 A1
CW/SHV CW2 ....41 E3
NANT CW5 ....38 B4
SBCH CW11 ....13 E2
Crewe Rd *ALS/KID* ST7 ....26 A4
ALS/KID ST7 ....3 K6
CW/SHV CW2 ....40 D1
NANT CW5 ....30 C4
SBCH CW11 ....14 A2
Crewe St *CW/HAS* CW1 ....3 C3
Crisham Av *NANT* CW5 ....38 B5
Crofters Cl *CW/SHV* CW2 ......31 G2
Cromer Dr *CW/HAS* CW1 ....11 G4
Cromwell Dr *CW/HAS* CW1 ....40 D2
Cronkinson Av *NANT* CW5 ......38 C1
Cronkinson Oak *NANT* CW5 ....38 C1
Crosslands *CW/HAS* CW1 ......23 C3
Cross La *CW/HAS* CW1 ....4 B3
SBCH CW11 ....4 B3
Cross Rd *CW/HAS* CW1 ....3 C5
Cross St *ALS/KID* ST7 ....26 B4
CW/HAS CW1 ....23 C3
CW/SHV CW2 ....3 G4
Crossway *CW/HAS* CW1 ....22 A1
Crossways Rd *ALS/KID* ST7 ......17 F3
Cross Wood St *NANT* * CW5 ....29 E5
Crotia Av *CW/HAS* CW1 ....33 E5
Crown Bank *SBCH* CW11 ....8 C3
Crown Ms *NANT* * CW5 ....29 F5
Cuckoo La *NANT* CW5 ....28 A2
Culland St *CW/HAS* CW1 ....3 F7
Cumberland Av *NANT* CW5 ....29 G4
Cumberland Cl *CW/HAS* CW1 ..22 A2
Cumbermere Dr *SBCH* CW11 ....7 H2
Curzon Av *ALS/KID* ST7 ....26 C2

Daisybank Dr *SBCH* CW11 ....8 D3
Dalton Ct *SBCH* CW11 ....7 H2
Dane Bank Av *CW/SHV* CW2 ....2 A7
Dane Cl *ALS/KID* ST7 ....25 H4
SBCH CW11 ....7 H2
Dane Pl *CW/HAS* CW1 ....22 A1
Dappleheath Rd *CW/SHV* CW2 ..31 F1
Darley Av *CW/SHV* CW2 ....2 A5
Darlington Av *CW/HAS* CW1 ....21 E2
Dart Cl *ALS/KID* ST7 ....25 H3
Davenham Crs *CW/HAS* CW1 ....21 E4
Davenport Av *CW/SHV* CW2 ....31 H2
NANT CW5 ....29 F4
Davenport Cl *SBCH* CW11..........9 E1
Davenport St *CW/HAS* CW1 ....21 H1
Davis Cl *ALS/KID* ST7 ....26 D3
Dean Cl *SBCH* CW11 ....7 H1
Deans La *SBCH* CW11 ....7 H3
Dee Cl *SBCH* CW11 ....7 H1
Delamere Cl *SBCH* CW11..........8 A1
Delamere Ct *ALS/KID* ST7 ......25 G3
Delamere Rd *NANT* CW5 ....38 B2
Delamere St *CW/HAS* CW1 ......2 E3
Delves Cl *CW/SHV* CW2 ....40 C1
Deneside Av *CW/HAS* CW1 ....21 H1
Denford Pl *ALS/KID* ST7 ....26 C1
Denston Cl *CW/SHV* CW2 ......31 C1
Denver Av *CW/SHV* CW2 ....2 D5
Derrington Av *CW/SHV* CW2 ....3 F5
Derwent Cl *ALS/KID* ST7 ......25 H3
NANT CW5 ....30 C4
Deva Rd *CW/SHV* CW2 ....2 D1
Dewes St *CW/HAS* CW1..........3 D1
Dickens Cl *SBCH* CW11 ....7 G3
Dig La *NANT* CW5 ....36 C1
NANT CW5 ....40 C5
Dillors Cft *CW/HAS* CW1 ......11 F3
The Dingle *CW/HAS* CW1 ......23 G2
Dingle La *SBCH* CW11 ....8 D3
Doddington Dr *SBCH* CW11 ......8 D2
Doddington Rd *CW/SHV* CW2 ..2 A5
Dog La *NANT* CW5 ....29 F4
Dorfold Cl *SBCH* CW11 ....8 D2
Dorfold Dr *NANT* CW5 ....29 E5
Dorfold St *CW/HAS* CW1 ....3 F3
Dorric Wy *CW/HAS* CW1 ....11 H5
Dove Cl *SBCH* CW11 ....8 B1
Dovecote Cl *CW/SHV* CW2 ......31 G2
Drake La *NANT* CW5 ....36 D1
Drayton Crs *CW/HAS* CW1 ......22 C2
Drovers Wy *SBCH* CW11 ....8 B4
Drury Cl *CW/HAS* CW1 ....22 C2
Drury La *CW/HAS* CW1 ....6 A5
Dryden Cl *CW/SHV* CW2 ....31 F2
Duchy Rd *CW/HAS* CW1 ....32 D2
Duke's Crs *SBCH* CW11 ....8 B1
Duke St *CW/HAS* CW1 ....3 C4
Dunham Cl *ALS/KID* ST7 ......26 B4
SBCH CW11 ....8 D3
Dunham Crs *CW/SHV* CW2 ....31 G2
Dunnilow Fld *NANT* CW5........38 D1
Dunnocksfold Rd *ALS/KID* ST7...25 G3
Dunnockswood *ALS/KID* ST7 ..25 H3
Dunwood Dr *ALS/KID* ST7 ......26 C1
Dunwoody Wy *CW/HAS* CW1 ....2 B1
Dutton Wy *CW/HAS* CW1 ......21 C1
NANT CW5 ....38 B2
Dysart Buildings *NANT* * CW5 ..29 F5

Eadie Gv *CW/HAS* CW1 ....11 F5
Eardswick La *CW/HAS* CW1 ......4 C5
Earle St *CW/HAS* CW1 ....3 C2
Earls Rd *CW/SHV* CW2 ....40 C1
East Av *CW/SHV* CW2 ....33 F5
East Ct *ALS/KID* ST7 ....26 A1
Eastern Rd *NANT* CW5............30 D5
East Vw *NANT* CW5 ....29 F4
Eaton Cl *SBCH* CW11 ....8 D2
Eaton Rd *ALS/KID* ST7 ....26 B3
Eaton St *CW/SHV* CW2 ....3 F4
Edgewood Dr *CW/SHV* CW2....31 F3
Edinburgh Rd *CW/SHV* CW2 ....30 D2
Edleston Hall La *NANT* CW5 ....36 D3
Edleston Rd *CW/HAS* CW1 ......3 C4
Edmund Wright Wy *NANT* CW5 ...28 D5
Edwards Av *CW/SHV* CW2 ......31 H5
Edwards Cl *CW/SHV* CW2 ......31 G5
Edward St *CW/SHV* CW2 ....3 G7
Edwards Wy *ALS/KID* ST7 ......26 D3
Elandor Rd *SBCH* CW11............7 G2
Elanor Rd *SBCH* CW11............7 G2
Eleanor Cl *CW/HAS* CW1 ....21 E2
Electra Wy *CW/HAS* CW1 ......22 C5
Electricity St *CW/SHV* CW2 ......3 F4

Eliot Cl *CW/HAS* CW1 22
Elizabeth St *CW/HAS* CW1 21
Ellesmere Cl *SBCH* CW11..........7
Ellesmere Pl *CW/HAS* CW1 21
Ellis St *CW/HAS* CW1 21
Ellwood Gn *CW/SHV* CW2 41
Elm Cl *CW/SHV* CW2............20
Elm Dr *CW/HAS* CW1 22
Elm Gv *ALS/KID* ST7 22
Elmstead Crs *CW/HAS* CW1 11
Elm Ter *CW/HAS* CW1 7
Elm Tree La *SBCH* CW11............7
Elmwood Cl *ALS/KID* ST7 27
Elsby Rd *ALS/KID* ST7............27
Elton Crossings Rd *SBCH* CW11...7
Elton La *SBCH* CW11 13
Elton Rd *SBCH* CW11 7
Elwood Wy *SBCH* CW11............7
Elworth Rd *SBCH* CW11 7
Elworth St *SBCH* CW11 7
Empress Dr *CW/SHV* CW2 2
Enfield Cl *CW/SHV* CW2..........31
Englefield Cl *CW/HAS* CW1 11
Englesea Gv *SBCH* CW11 31
Ennerdale Rd *CW/SHV* CW2 20
Ernest St *CW/HAS* CW1 7
Etherow Cl *SBCH* CW11............7
Ettiley Av *SBCH* CW11............7
Evans St *CW/HAS* CW1 21
Eva St *SBCH* CW11 7

F

Fairbrook *CW/SHV* CW2 20
Fairburn Av *CW/SHV* CW2 21
Fairfield Av *SBCH* CW11 8
Fairview Av *ALS/KID* ST7........26
CW/SHV CW2 33
The Fairway *ALS/KID* ST7 26
Falcon Dr *CW/HAS* CW1 11
Fallowfield Ct *CW/HAS* CW1 21
Falmouth Rd *CW/HAS* CW1 21
Fanny's Cft *ALS/KID* ST7 27
Fanshawe Wk *CW/SHV* CW2 31
Farams Rd *ALS/KID* ST7..........7
Farmer Cl *CW/SHV* CW2 20
Farmleigh Dr *CW/HAS* CW1 11
Farndale Av *CW/SHV* CW2 33
Fernbank Cl *CW/HAS* CW1 22
Fern Ct *CW/HAS* CW1 7
Ferndale Ct *CW/SHV* CW2 33
SBCH CW11 8
Fernleaf Cl *ALS/KID* ST7 17
The Fields *NANT* CW5 30
Field Av *CW/SHV* CW2 31
Field La *CW/SHV* CW2 31
Fields Cl *ALS/KID* ST7 26
Fields Dr *SBCH* CW11..............8
Fields Rd *ALS/KID* ST7 26
CW/HAS CW1 23
Fields View Cl *NANT* CW5 40
Field Wy *ALS/KID* ST7............27
Firbeck Gdns *CW/SHV* CW2 20
First Av *CW/HAS* CW1 3
SBCH CW11 8
First Dig La *NANT* CW5 39
First Wood St *NANT* CW5 29
Firwood Wk *CW/SHV* CW2 31
Fishermans Cl *CW/HAS* CW1 7
Flag La *CW/HAS* CW1..............2
Flamingo Cl *CW/HAS* CW1 11
Flat La *CW/HAS* CW11..............8
Fletcher St *CW/HAS* CW1 21
Flixton Dr *CW/SHV* CW2 2
Flowers La *CW/HAS* CW1 10
Foden Av *ALS/KID* ST7............27
Ford Cl *CW/HAS* CW1 21
Ford La *CW/HAS* CW1 21
Forge Flds *SBCH* CW11 14
Forge St *CW/HAS* CW1 3
Foulkes Av *CW/HAS* CW1 22
Foundry La *SBCH* CW11 7
Fountain Cottages *SBCH* * CW11...14
Fourseasons Cl *CW/SHV* CW2 ..31
Fourth Av *CW/HAS* CW1 32
Fourways *CW/HAS* CW1 7
Foxes Hollow *CW/HAS* CW1 12
Foxglove Cl *CW/SHV* CW2 20
Frances St *CW/HAS* CW1 3
Frank Bott Av *CW/HAS* CW1 11
Franklyn Av *CW/HAS* CW1........3
Frank Webb Av *CW/HAS* CW1 ..21
Freshfields *CW/SHV* CW2 3
Front St *SBCH* CW11................7
Fulbeck Cl *CW/SHV* CW2 31
Fuller Dr *CW/SHV* CW2 31

Manor Av CW/SHV CW2 ...31 F1
Manor Ct CW/SHV CW2 ...31 G1
Manor Gdns NANT CW5 ...29 F4
Manor Rd NANT CW5 ...29 F4
   SBCH CW11 ...9 E5
Manor Rd North NANT CW5 ...29 F4
Manor Wy CW/SHV CW2 ...31 G1
   SBCH CW11 ...9 F5
Mansion Ct NANT * CW5 ...29 G5
Maple Av ALS/KID ST7 ...26 D5
Maple Cl SBCH CW11 ...8 D3
Maple Gv CW/HAS CW1 ...22 B1
Maple Pl ALS/KID ST7 ...17 E5
March St CW/HAS CW1 ...3 H2
Market Sq CW/HAS CW1 ...3 F3
Market St CW/HAS CW1 ...3 G2
   NANT CW5 ...29 F4
Marlborough Cl CW/SHV CW2 ...30 D2
Marley Av CW/SHV CW2 ...21 C1
Marlowe Cl CW/SHV CW2 ...31 F2
   SBCH CW11 ...7 F4
Marlowe Dr NANT CW5 ...38 B2
Marple Crs CW/SHV CW2 ...20 D5
Marriott Rd SBCH CW11 ...14 A1
Marsh Cl ALS/KID ST7 ...25 H4
Marshfield Av CW/SHV CW2 ...20 C2
Marshfield Bank CW/SHV CW2 ...20 C3
Marsh Green Rd SBCH CW11 ...7 G1
Marsh La ALS/KID ST7 ...25 H4
   NANT CW5 ...37 E2
Marton Cl CW/SHV CW2 ...41 F2
Marys Ga CW/SHV CW2 ...30 D2
Mary St CW/HAS CW1 ...3 H2
Masefield Dr CW/HAS CW1 ...22 C3
Masefield Wy CW/HAS CW11 ...7 G4
Mavor Ct CW/HAS CW1 ...2 D2
Mawdsley Cl ALS/KID ST7 ...25 G4
Maw Green Cl CW/HAS CW1 ...12 B5
Maw Green Rd CW/HAS CW1 ...12 C5
Maw La CW/HAS CW1 ...12 D5
Maxwell St CW/SHV CW2 ...3 F5
Mayfield Ms CW/HAS CW1 ...21 E1
Mayflower Rd NANT CW5 ...38 B1
Mclaren St CW/HAS CW1 ...11 G5
Mcneill Av CW/HAS CW1 ...21 E2
Meadow Av CW/SHV CW2 ...33 E5
Meadow Cl CW/SHV CW2 ...32 A5
Meadow Cft ALS/KID ST7 ...26 D5
Meadow Dr CW/SHV CW2 ...31 E5
Meadowgate Cl SBCH CW11 ...7 G4
Meadowvale NANT CW5 ...29 F5
Meadow Wy ALS/KID ST7 ...27 F2
Meads Rd ALS/KID ST7 ...26 C3
Meeanee Dr NANT CW5 ...38 A1
Melbourne Gv CW/HAS CW1 ...23 F2
Melford Dr CW/SHV CW2 ...31 H2
Mellor St CW/HAS CW1 ...22 A2
Melrose Dr CW/HAS CW1 ...11 F4
Mercer Wy NANT CW5 ...29 F3
Mercian Cl CW/SHV CW2 ...40 C1
Merebank Rd CW/SHV CW2 ...31 G1
Mere Brook Wk CW/SHV CW2 ...31 H1
Mere Cl CW/HAS CW1 ...23 G3
Meredith St CW/HAS CW1 ...2 E1
Mere Rd CW/SHV CW2 ...33 E5
Mere St CW/HAS CW1 ...23 G3
Merganser Cl CW/HAS CW1 ...11 E5
Merlin Wy CW/HAS CW1 ...11 F4
Merrill's Av CW/SHV CW2 ...20 D1
Merrivale Rd CW/SHV CW2 ...31 G2
Meynell Cl CW/SHV CW2 ...31 F1
Micklewright Av CW/HAS CW1 ...22 A2
Middlewich Rd CW/HAS CW1 ...10 D5
   CW/SHV CW2 ...20 B4
   MWCH CW10 ...4 D1
   NANT CW5 ...29 G3
   SBCH CW11 ...7 H3
Middlewich St CW/HAS CW1 ...22 A2
Millbeck Cl CW/SHV CW2 ...33 E5
Mill Bridge Cl CW/HAS CW1 ...22 C4
Millbuck Wy SBCH CW11 ...7 F3
Millers Whf ALS/KID ST7 ...16 D5
Millfields NANT CW5 ...38 A1
Mill Hill Dr SBCH CW11 ...8 B5
Mill Hill La SBCH CW11 ...8 B5
Mill La CW/SHV CW2 ...32 D4
   CW/SHV CW2 ...34 D3
   SBCH CW11 ...14 B2
Millmead ALS/KID ST7 ...17 E5
Millrace Dr CW/SHV CW2 ...31 G2
Mill Rw SBCH CW11 ...8 D3
Millstone La NANT CW5 ...29 G5
Mill St CW/SHV CW2 ...3 G4
   NANT CW5 ...29 F5
Mills Wy CW/HAS CW1 ...11 G4
Mill Wy NANT CW5 ...38 C3
Milne Cl CW/SHV CW2 ...31 E2
Milton Dr CW/SHV CW2 ...31 E2

Milton Wy SBCH CW11 ...7 G3
Minshull New Rd CW/HAS CW1 ...21 E1
Minster St CW/HAS CW1 ...3 H2
Mirion St CW/HAS CW1 ...3 H2
Moat House Dr CW/SHV CW2 ...2 B7
Monarch Cl CW/SHV CW2 ...21 E3
Monks La CW/HAS CW1 ...21 E1
   NANT CW5 ...28 A3
   NANT CW5 ...29 F5
Monks Orch NANT CW5 ...29 G5
Monk St CW/HAS CW1 ...2 B1
Montrose Cl CW/SHV CW2 ...40 C2
Moorfields NANT CW5 ...30 D4
Moorhouse Av ALS/KID ST7 ...26 B5
Moorlands Dr NANT CW5 ...40 B5
Moreton Dr ALS/KID ST7 ...26 A4
   SBCH CW11 ...8 D2
Moreton Rd CW/SHV CW2 ...21 E5
Morgan Cl CW/SHV CW2 ...2 A2
Mornington Cl SBCH CW11 ...7 G2
Mortimer Dr SBCH CW11 ...8 D4
Moss Cft CW/HAS CW1 ...11 F4
Mossdale Cl CW/SHV CW2 ...18 A3
Moss Flds ALS/KID ST7 ...25 H4
Mossford Av CW/HAS CW1 ...11 G5
Moss La CW/HAS CW1 ...10 D2
   NANT CW5 ...40 B4
   SBCH CW11 ...7 F2
Moss Sq CW/HAS CW1 ...3 G3
Moss Wy ALS/KID ST7 ...25 H4
Moston Rd SBCH CW11 ...7 F4
Mountbatten Ct CW/SHV CW2 ...2 B4
Mount Cl NANT CW5 ...29 G4
Mount Dr NANT CW5 ...29 G4
Mount Pleasant CW/HAS CW1 ...21 G1
   CW/HAS CW1 ...23 G3
Mulberry Gdns SBCH CW11 ...7 G2
Mulberry Rd CW/SHV CW2 ...20 D5
Mulcaster Ct CW/HAS CW1 ...23 G2
Murrayfield Dr NANT CW5 ...30 C5
Myrtle St CW/SHV CW2 ...3 F5

N

Nantwich Rd NANT CW5 ...20 B5
Narrow La CW/HAS CW1 ...23 F4
Needhams Bank SBCH CW11 ...7 F3
Nelson Gv ALS/KID ST7 ...27 E5
Nelson St CW/SHV CW2 ...3 F6
Nesfield Ct SBCH CW11 ...13 H5
Nesfield Dr CW/HAS CW1 ...14 A5
Nessina Gv CW/SHV CW2 ...31 E2
Neville St CW/SHV CW2 ...32 A1
Nevis Dr CW/SHV CW2 ...20 C4
Newbold Wy NANT CW5 ...38 B2
Newbury Av CW/HAS CW1 ...11 H5
Newcastle Rd CW/SHV CW2 ...40 C2
   NANT CW5 ...39 E1
   NANT CW5 ...9 G5
Newcastle St CW/HAS CW1 ...21 F2
Newdigate St CW/HAS CW1 ...3 F1
Newfield Dr CW/HAS CW1 ...22 B2
Newfield St SBCH CW11 ...8 C2
Newhall Av SBCH CW11 ...8 B4
New Inn La SBCH CW11 ...15 H2
Newland Wy NANT CW5 ...39 E1
Newman's La CW/HAS CW1 ...39 G5
New St CW/HAS CW1 ...23 F2
   SBCH CW11 ...7 G2
Newtons Crs CW/HAS CW1 ...13 H5
Newtons La CW/HAS CW1 ...13 H5
Newton St CW/HAS CW1 ...3 G1
Nigel Gresley Cl CW/HAS CW1 ...22 D3
Nightingale Cl CW/HAS CW1 ...11 E5
Nile St CW/SHV CW2 ...3 F6
Nixon's Rw NANT CW5 ...28 D5
Nixon St CW/HAS CW1 ...21 E2
Norbreck Av CW/SHV CW2 ...2 D7
Norbury Cl CW/HAS CW1 ...41 F2
Northbank Wk CW/SHV CW2 ...31 H2
North Cft NANT CW5 ...29 F5
Northfield Pl CW/SHV CW2 ...31 H1
North Stafford St CW/HAS CW1 ...3 H2
North St CW/HAS CW1 ...11 H5
North Wy CW/SHV CW2 ...32 A5
Norton Wy SBCH CW11 ...7 G2
Nova Ct CW/HAS * CW1 ...2 D1
Nursery Rd CW/HAS CW1 ...25 E5
Nutfield Av CW/SHV CW2 ...11 G5
Nuthurst Gdns NANT CW5 ...29 G5

O

Oak Av ALS/KID ST7 ...26 D5
Oak Bank Cl NANT CW5 ...39 H1
Oakdene Ct SBCH * CW11 ...8 C3
Oak Gv NANT CW5 ...38 B2
Oakhurst Dr CW/SHV CW2 ...31 C5
Oakland Av CW/HAS CW1 ...23 F3
Oakley Cl SBCH CW11 ...8 B1
Oakley St CW/HAS CW1 ...3 F1
Oakmere Cl SBCH CW11 ...8 A1
Oak St ALS/KID ST7 ...16 D4
   CW/SHV CW2 ...3 G4
   SBCH CW11 ...7 G1
Oak Tree Cl CW/HAS CW1 ...22 C2
Oak Tree Dr CW/HAS CW1 ...22 C2
Oakwood Crs CW/SHV CW2 ...20 D3
   SBCH CW11 ...9 F3
Oakwood La SBCH CW11 ...7 G1
Oat Market NANT CW5 ...28 D4
Offley Av SBCH CW11 ...8 C2
Offley Rd SBCH CW11 ...8 C2
Oldfield Rd SBCH CW11 ...14 A1
Old Gorse Cl CW/SHV CW2 ...20 D4
Old Mill Rd SBCH CW11 ...8 D3
Old Park Rd CW/HAS CW1 ...33 G3
The Orchards CW/SHV CW2 ...40 D1
Orchard Ct CW/HAS CW1 ...23 G2
Orchard Crs NANT CW5 ...38 B2
Orchard St CW/HAS CW1 ...2 E1
   NANT CW5 ...30 C4
Ordsall Cl SBCH CW11 ...14 A1
Ormerod Cl SBCH CW11 ...8 A1
Osborne Cl SBCH CW11 ...7 G4
Osborne Gv CW/SHV CW2 ...40 D1
Ossmere Cl SBCH CW11 ...8 A1
Owen St CW/SHV CW2 ...2 E6
Oxford St CW/HAS CW1 ...2 C1

P

The Paddock NANT CW5 ...39 G4
   SBCH CW11 ...15 G3
Padston Dr ALS/KID ST7 ...25 H4
Padstow St CW/HAS CW1 ...11 H4
Padworth Pl CW/HAS CW1 ...11 G5
Page Gv CW/SHV CW2 ...40 C2
Pall Ml NANT CW5 ...29 F5
Palmer Rd SBCH CW11 ...8 D4
Palmerston Cl CW/HAS CW1 ...23 F2
Parish Cl ALS/KID ST7 ...26 A3
Park Dr CW/SHV CW2 ...31 E1
Parkers Rd CW/HAS CW1 ...11 F4
Park Est CW/HAS CW1 ...32 A5
Parkfield CW/HAS CW1 ...11 F4
Parkfield Dr NANT CW5 ...38 B1
Park House Dr SBCH CW11 ...8 D1
Park La ALS/KID ST7 ...35 H5
   SBCH CW11 ...8 A3
Park Rd CW/HAS CW1 ...23 G2
   NANT CW5 ...30 B5
   NANT CW5 ...38 B2
Parkstone Dr CW/HAS CW1 ...11 G4
Park Vw NANT CW5 ...29 G4
Patterdale Cl CW/SHV CW2 ...20 C4
Peach La NANT CW5 ...29 H1
Pear Tree Av CW/HAS CW1 ...11 G5
Peartree Cl SBCH CW11 ...9 F3
Pear Tree Fld NANT CW5 ...38 D1
Peckforton Cl SBCH CW11 ...7 H2
Pedley St CW/SHV CW2 ...3 H6
Peel Sq CW/HAS CW1 ...2 C1
Peel St CW/HAS CW1 ...2 C1
Pelham Cl CW/HAS CW1 ...23 F2
Pelican Cl CW/HAS CW1 ...22 C2
Penbrook Cl CW/SHV CW2 ...20 C4
Pendle Cl CW/HAS CW1 ...22 D2
Penlington Ct NANT CW5 ...29 G4
Pepper St NANT CW5 ...29 F5
Percy James Cl ALS/KID ST7 ...26 D3
Peter Pl CW/HAS CW1 ...2 D1
Petworth Cl CW/SHV CW2 ...31 G2
Pickmere Cl SBCH CW11 ...8 A2
Pickmere Ct CW/HAS CW1 ...21 H2
Pickwick Cl SBCH CW11 ...8 D1
Pikemere Rd ALS/KID ST7 ...26 A2
The Pike NANT CW5 ...38 B2
Pillory St NANT CW5 ...29 F5
Pine Gv SBCH CW11 ...8 D3
Pine Wk NANT CW5 ...38 B1
Pinewood Cl CW/SHV CW2 ...31 G3
Pit La CW/SHV CW2 ...41 F3
Plane Tree Dr CW/HAS CW1 ...22 B1
Plant St SBCH CW11 ...8 B2

Platt Av SBCH CW11 ...8
The Plex ALS/KID ST7 ...26
Plough Cft ALS/KID ST7 ...25
Pollard Dr NANT CW5 ...39
Poole Old Hall La NANT CW5 ...18
Pool La SBCH CW11 ...14
Pool Side ALS/KID ST7 ...17
Pool Vw CW/HAS CW1 ...14
The Poplars CW/SHV CW2 ...31
Poplar Dr ALS/KID ST7 ...26
Poplar Gv CW/HAS CW1 ...3
Poppyfields ALS/KID ST7 ...26
Portland Gv CW/HAS CW1 ...3
Potter Cl NANT CW5 ...39
Pratchitts Rw NANT * CW5 ...29
The Precinct CW/SHV * CW2 ...21
Preece Ct CW/HAS CW1 ...2
Price Av SBCH CW11 ...8
Price Dr SBCH CW11 ...8
Priestley Ct NANT * CW5 ...29
Primrose Av CW/SHV CW2 ...23
Primrose Hl CW/SHV CW2 ...20
Prince Albert St CW/HAS CW1 ...3
Prince Edward St NANT CW5 ...29
Princess Cl CW/SHV CW2 ...31
Princess Dr CW/SHV CW2 ...30
   NANT CW5 ...29
   SBCH CW11 ...8
Princess Gv CW/SHV CW2 ...31
Princess St CW/HAS CW1 ...21
Prior Cl CW/SHV CW2 ...31
Priory Cl CW/SHV CW2 ...11
Probert Cl CW/SHV CW2 ...2
Proctors La SBCH CW11 ...7
Prunus Rd CW/HAS CW1 ...22
Pym's La CW/HAS CW1 ...20
Pyrus Av CW/HAS CW1 ...22

Q

Quakers Coppice CW/HAS CW1 ...22
Queen's Crs CW/HAS CW1 ...10
Queen's Dr NANT CW5 ...37
   SBCH CW11 ...8
Queen's Park Dr CW/SHV CW2 ...21
Queen's Park Gdns CW/SHV CW2 ...20
Queen St CW/HAS CW1 ...3
   CW/SHV CW2 ...40
Queensway ALS/KID ST7 ...26
   CW/HAS CW1 ...3

R

Radbroke Cl SBCH CW11 ...9
Radcliffe Rd SBCH CW11 ...14
Radnor Cl SBCH CW11 ...7
Radway Green Rd CW/SHV CW2 ...34
Railbrook Ct CW/SHV * CW2 ...3
Railton Av CW/HAS CW1 ...11
Railway St CW/HAS CW1 ...3
Rainbow St CW/HAS CW1 ...3
Ramsbottom St CW/HAS CW1 ...2
Raven Cl SBCH CW11 ...8
Ravenscroft Cl SBCH CW11 ...8
Ravenscroft Rd CW/SHV CW2 ...20
Ravens La NANT CW5 ...36
Ray Av NANT CW5 ...29
Readesdale Av CW/SHV CW2 ...21
Rectory Cl CW/SHV CW2 ...30
   NANT CW5 ...29
Redesmere Cl SBCH CW11 ...8
Red La SBCH CW11 ...7
Red Lion La NANT CW5 ...29
Regent Cl CW/SHV CW2 ...40
Regents Ga NANT CW5 ...29
Reid St CW/HAS CW1 ...21
Remer St CW/HAS CW1 ...12
Renaissance Cl CW/HAS CW1 ...22
Renaissance Wy CW/SHV CW2 ...23
Repton Dr CW/HAS CW1 ...23
The Retreat CW/HAS CW1 ...21
Reynold's La SBCH CW11 ...9
Rhoden St CW/HAS CW1 ...22
Rhodes Cl CW/HAS CW1 ...23
Richard Moon St CW/HAS CW1 ...2
Richardson Cl CW/HAS CW1 ...23
   SBCH CW11 ...7
Richard St CW/HAS CW1 ...3
Richmond Cl SBCH CW11 ...9
Richmond Rd CW/HAS CW1 ...3
Riddings La NANT CW5 ...40
Ridgway St CW/HAS CW1 ...2
Ridley Cl CW/SHV CW2 ...41
Rigby Av CW/HAS CW1 ...11

ys Rw NANT CW5 ..... 29 F5
g St CW/HAS CW1 ..... 2 D1
y Cl SBCH CW11 ..... 7 G4
sdale Cl CW/SHV CW2 ..... 31 F5
on Dr CW/SHV CW2 ..... 31 F2
erbank Cl NANT CW5 ..... 29 F3
erpark Cl NANT CW5 ..... 29 F2
erside NANT CW5 ..... 29 E5
erside Gv CW/SHV CW2 ..... 20 C4
in Cl SBCH CW11 ..... 8 B1
hester Crs CW/HAS CW1 ..... 22 C1
kwood Av CW/SHV CW2 ..... 2 B4
e House Cl ALS/KID ST7 ..... 17 E5
e Rode ALS/KID ST7 ..... 26 C3
buck St CW/HAS CW1 ..... 2 E1
dean Wk CW/HAS CW1 ..... 22 A1
s Av CW/HAS CW1 ..... 21 F1
nan Wy SBCH CW11 ..... 7 H2
kery Cl NANT CW5 ..... 29 G5
CH CW11 ..... 7 F4
kery Dr NANT CW5 ..... 38 B1
k St CW/SHV CW2 ..... 2 E6
e Bank Av CW/SHV CW2 ..... 31 F3
e La CW/SHV CW2 ..... 31 F3
ebery Wy CW/HAS CW1 ..... 23 F3
ehill Rd CW/SHV CW2 ..... 31 F1
e Ter CW/HAS CW1 ..... 21 H2
ewood Cl CW/HAS * CW1 ..... 22 B1
therne Wy SBCH CW11 ..... 8 A2
ghwood La SBCH CW11 ..... 15 H3
van Cl ALS/KID ST7 ..... 26 C4
S/KID ST7 ..... 26 B1
CH CW11 ..... 8 A3
ton Rd CW/SHV CW2 ..... 20 C3
al Ar CW/HAS CW1 ..... 3 F2
ce Cl CW/HAS CW1 ..... 11 F5
heath Cl CW/SHV CW2 ..... 20 C2
ord Cl CW/SHV CW2 ..... 31 G2
coe Av SBCH CW11 ..... 7 H3
hton Dr CW/SHV CW2 ..... 41 F3
kin Rd CW/SHV CW2 ..... 2 E7
sell Av ALS/KID ST7 ..... 26 B2
sell Dr CW/HAS CW1 ..... 23 F2
land Cl SBCH CW11 ..... 7 F4
al Mt CW/HAS CW1 ..... 11 G3
al Wy ALS/KID ST7 ..... 26 B2
CH CW11 ..... 11 G4
bank Av CW/HAS CW1 ..... 11 G5
Cl ALS/KID ST7 ..... 26 A4

S

lbans Dr NANT CW5 ..... 38 C2
ndrew's Av CW/SHV CW2 ..... 31 H1
ndrews Gdns ALS/KID ST7 ..... 26 D5
nne's La CW/HAS CW1 ..... 29 E5
hads Cl NANT CW5 ..... 40 B5
lairs St CW/SHV CW2 ..... 32 A1
rewood Cl CW/SHV CW2 ..... 31 G3
abriels Ct ALS/KID ST7 ..... 26 B4
ohn's Wy SBCH CW11 ..... 9 F3
osephs Wy NANT CW5 ..... 29 H5
awrence Ct NANT CW5 ..... 29 G4
larys Cl ALS/KID ST7 ..... 26 B2
larys Ct NANT CW5 ..... 28 B3
lary's St CW/HAS CW1 ..... 29 F3
lary's St CW/HAS CW1 ..... 2 E1
latthews Cl CW/HAS CW1 ..... 23 G3
aul's Ct CW/HAS CW1 ..... 2 E2
aul's St CW/HAS CW1 ..... 2 E1
eter's Ri SBCH CW11 ..... 7 H2
tephens Ct SBCH CW11 ..... 7 G2
ander Crs CW/SHV CW2 ..... 31 F3
sbury Av CW/SHV CW2 ..... 31 H1
sbury Cl CW/SHV CW2 ..... 31 H1
Line Wy SBCH CW11 ..... 7 G3
Mdw NANT CW5 ..... 28 D5
uel St CW/HAS CW1 ..... 2 D1
dbach Rd ALS/KID ST7 ..... 26 C1
CH CW11 ..... 16 C3
dbach Rd North ALS/KID ST7 ..... 26 B2
dbach Rd South ALS/KID ST7 ..... 26 C4
derson Cl CW/SHV CW2 ..... 31 H2
dford Rd NANT CW5 ..... 29 G3
dhurst Av CW/SHV CW2 ..... 31 F1
diway Rd CW/HAS CW1 ..... 21 F1
don Park Gdns CW/SHV CW2 ..... 20 C3
don St CW/HAS CW1 ..... 3 G5
down Rd CW/HAS CW1 ..... 11 H5
dpiper Cl CW/HAS CW1 ..... 11 G5
dringham Dr CW/SHV CW2 ..... 30 D3
dside Rd ALS/KID ST7 ..... 25 H4
dylands Crs ALS/KID ST7 ..... 27 E2
dylands Pk CW/SHV CW2 ..... 30 C3
dy La SBCH CW11 ..... 7 G4
CH CW11 ..... 14 B5

Saunders St CW/HAS CW1 ..... 2 D2
Savoy Rd CW/HAS CW1 ..... 32 D2
Scaife St NANT CW5 ..... 29 F5
School Crs CW/HAS CW1 ..... 3 K3
School La NANT CW5 ..... 29 F4
  SBCH CW11 ..... 6 A2
  SBCH CW11 ..... 7 G2
  SBCH CW11 ..... 9 F3
School St CW/HAS CW1 ..... 23 G2
Scott Av CW/HAS CW1 ..... 22 C3
Scott Cl ALS/KID ST7 ..... 16 D4
Seagull Cl CW/HAS CW1 ..... 22 C2
Seaton Cl CW/HAS CW1 ..... 11 G4
Second Av CW/HAS CW1 ..... 32 C1
  CW/HAS CW1 ..... 8 B4
Second Wood St NANT CW5 ..... 29 E5
Sedgmere Av CW/HAS CW1 ..... 11 G4
Selsey Cl CW/HAS CW1 ..... 11 G4
Selworthy Dr CW/HAS CW1 ..... 11 G5
Shady Gv ALS/KID ST7 ..... 26 C3
Shakespeare Dr CW/HAS CW1 ..... 22 D3
Shannon Cl NANT CW5 ..... 30 C5
Sharnbrook Dr CW/SHV CW2 ..... 20 D4
Shelburne Dr CW/HAS CW1 ..... 11 F2
Shelley Cl ALS/KID ST7 ..... 16 D4
  CW/HAS CW1 ..... 22 C3
Shelley Ct SBCH CW11 ..... 7 G3
Shelley Dr CW/SHV CW2 ..... 31 E1
Sheppard Cl CW/HAS CW1 ..... 3 H2
Sherborne Rd CW/HAS CW1 ..... 22 A1
Sheridan Cl CW/HAS CW1 ..... 11 G3
Sheringham Dr CW/HAS CW1 ..... 11 G3
Sherwin St CW/SHV CW2 ..... 3 F7
Shrewbridge Crs NANT CW5 ..... 29 F5
Shrewbridge Rd NANT CW5 ..... 38 A3
Simpson Ct CW/HAS CW1 ..... 11 G3
Sinclair Av ALS/KID ST7 ..... 26 A4
Singleton Av CW/HAS CW1 ..... 21 H1
Skeath Cl SBCH CW11 ..... 9 E3
Skylark Cl CW/HAS CW1 ..... 11 E5
Smallbrook Wk CW/SHV CW2 ..... 31 H1
Smallman Rd CW/HAS CW1 ..... 31 H1
Smith Cl ALS/KID ST7 ..... 26 A3
Smithfield La SBCH CW11 ..... 8 D3
Smith Gv CW/HAS CW1 ..... 21 E1
Smithy La CW/HAS CW1 ..... 10 D4
  CW/SHV CW2 ..... 33 F5
  CW/SHV CW2 ..... 34 D4
Smithy Wk SBCH CW11 ..... 14 A1
Snape Rd CW/SHV CW2 ..... 32 A2
Snowdon Dr CW/SHV CW2 ..... 20 C4
Somerford Av CW/HAS CW1 ..... 2 A5
Somerford Cl SBCH CW11 ..... 8 D1
Somerley Cl CW/HAS CW1 ..... 11 G4
Somerville St CW/SHV CW2 ..... 2 D7
Sorbus Dr CW/HAS CW1 ..... 22 B1
South Av CW/HAS CW1 ..... 23 G3
Southbank Av CW/HAS CW1 ..... 31 H5
South Cheshire Wy ALS/KID ST7 ..... 16 D3
  ALS/KID ST7 ..... 41 G3
South Crofts NANT CW5 ..... 29 F5
Southey Cl NANT CW5 ..... 29 F5
Southfields Cl NANT CW5 ..... 40 B5
South St CW/SHV CW2 ..... 3 H7
Spencer Cl ALS/KID ST7 ..... 25 G3
  CW/SHV CW2 ..... 31 F2
The Spinney NANT CW5 ..... 30 C4
  SBCH CW11 ..... 8 D3
Spinney Dr CW/HAS CW1 ..... 33 E5
Spring Cl ALS/KID ST7 ..... 16 D4
Springfield Dr CW/SHV CW2 ..... 31 E3
Spring Gdns CW/HAS CW1 ..... 3 J1
  NANT CW5 ..... 29 G5
Springwell Cl CW/SHV CW2 ..... 31 E3
Spruce Gv ALS/KID ST7 ..... 26 C3
Stafford St CW/HAS CW1 ..... 2 E1
Stalbridge Rd CW/SHV CW2 ..... 3 F6
Stamford Av CW/SHV CW2 ..... 2 E5
Stamp Av CW/HAS CW1 ..... 22 A1
Stanhope Av CW/HAS CW1 ..... 3 K5
Stanier Cl CW/HAS CW1 ..... 22 D3
Stanley Cl ALS/KID ST7 ..... 26 B3
Stanley St CW/HAS CW1 ..... 2 E2
Stannerhouse La SBCH CW11 ..... 15 H1
Stanthorne Av CW/HAS CW1 ..... 21 E4
Stapeley Cl CW/HAS CW1 ..... 31 G1
Stapeley Ter NANT CW5 ..... 38 D1
Station Rd ALS/KID ST7 ..... 26 B4
  NANT CW5 ..... 19 F1
  NANT CW5 ..... 29 F1
  SBCH CW11 ..... 7 G2
Station Vw NANT CW5 ..... 38 B1
Stephenson Dr CW/HAS CW1 ..... 22 D3
Sterne Cl SBCH CW11 ..... 7 G3
Stewart St CW/SHV CW2 ..... 2 B5
Stock La NANT CW5 ..... 40 B4
Stonebridge Rd NANT CW5 ..... 38 A2

Stonechat Cl CW/HAS CW1 ..... 11 E5
Stoneley Av CW/HAS CW1 ..... 11 H5
Stoneley Rd CW/HAS CW1 ..... 12 A5
Strathaven Av CW/SHV CW2 ..... 30 D2
Street La SBCH CW11 ..... 16 D2
Stringer Av SBCH CW11 ..... 8 D3
Sunart Cl CW/SHV CW2 ..... 31 F3
Sundale Dr CW/SHV CW2 ..... 20 C4
Sunnybank Rd CW/SHV CW2 ..... 20 D2
Sunnyside ALS/KID ST7 ..... 25 H5
Surrey St CW/HAS CW1 ..... 3 J2
Swallow Dr SBCH CW11 ..... 8 B1
Swallowfield Cl CW/SHV CW2 ..... 31 F2
Sweet Briar Crs CW/SHV CW2 ..... 21 E4
Sweettooth La SBCH CW11 ..... 8 B1
Swettenham Cl ALS/KID ST7 ..... 26 B4
  SBCH CW11 ..... 8 D2
Swift Cl CW/SHV CW2 ..... 31 E1
Swinburne Dr CW/HAS CW1 ..... 22 C3
Swine Market NANT CW5 ..... 29 E5
Swinnerton St CW/SHV CW2 ..... 3 F7
Sycamore Av ALS/KID ST7 ..... 17 E5
  ALS/KID ST7 ..... 26 D5
  CW/HAS CW1 ..... 22 A1
Sycamore Cl SBCH CW11 ..... 29 G3
Sycamore Gv SBCH CW11 ..... 8 B1
Sydney Rd CW/HAS CW1 ..... 22 B1

T

Tabley Cl SBCH CW11 ..... 7 H2
Tabley Rd CW/SHV CW2 ..... 20 D4
Tailors Vw NANT * CW5 ..... 29 F4
Talbot Cl CW/SHV CW2 ..... 40 C1
Talke Rd ALS/KID ST7 ..... 26 D4
Tame Cl SBCH CW11 ..... 7 H1
Tanners Wy NANT CW5 ..... 38 B1
Tarvin Av CW/SHV CW2 ..... 20 C3
Tate Dr CW/HAS CW1 ..... 23 F3
Tatton Cl ALS/KID * ST7 ..... 26 B4
Tatton Dr SBCH CW11 ..... 7 F3
Tatton Rd CW/SHV CW2 ..... 20 D5
Taxmere Cl SBCH CW11 ..... 8 A2
Taylor's La CW/HAS CW1 ..... 24 D4
Telford Gdns SBCH CW11 ..... 14 A1
Telford Pl NANT CW5 ..... 28 D5
Tenchersfield NANT CW5 ..... 38 D1
Tennyson Av CW/HAS CW1 ..... 22 C3
Tennyson Cl ALS/KID ST7 ..... 16 D4
  CW/SHV CW2 ..... 31 F1
Thackery Ct SBCH CW11 ..... 7 G3
Third Av CW/HAS CW1 ..... 32 C1
  SBCH CW11 ..... 8 B4
Thirlmere Rd CW/SHV CW2 ..... 31 E1
Thomas Cl ALS/KID ST7 ..... 26 D3
Thomas Rw NANT * CW5 ..... 29 F4
Thomas St CW/HAS CW1 ..... 3 G1
Thorley Gv CW/HAS CW1 ..... 31 F1
Thornbrook Wy SBCH CW11 ..... 7 G4
Thornton Dr CW/SHV CW2 ..... 31 F3
Thorn Tree Dr CW/HAS CW1 ..... 11 F3
Thorpe Cl CW/HAS CW1 ..... 11 E4
Tilstone Cl CW/SHV CW2 ..... 41 F3
Timbrell Av CW/HAS CW1 ..... 21 F1
Tiverton Cl SBCH CW11 ..... 8 D2
Tollemache Dr CW/HAS CW1 ..... 11 H3
Tollitt St CW/HAS CW1 ..... 3 F3
Tommy's La CW/HAS CW1 ..... 3 J6
Towers Cl CW/SHV CW2 ..... 31 F3
Tower Wy CW/HAS CW1 ..... 3 F3
Town Flds SBCH CW11 ..... 8 B4
Townsend La ALS/KID ST7 ..... 17 F4
Townwell Ct NANT * CW5 ..... 29 E5
Trevithick Cl CW/HAS CW1 ..... 22 D3
Tricketts La NANT CW5 ..... 30 D3
Trinity Cl CW/HAS CW1 ..... 31 F1
Tudor Wy NANT CW5 ..... 38 B2
Tunbridge Cl CW/SHV CW2 ..... 31 F2
Turner Cl CW/HAS CW1 ..... 11 F4
Turner St NANT CW5 ..... 29 G5
Twemlow Av SBCH CW11 ..... 8 C1
Tynedale Cl CW/SHV CW2 ..... 2 D7

U

Ullswater Av CW/SHV CW2 ..... 20 D4
Underwood La CW/HAS CW1 ..... 21 G2
Union St CW/SHV CW2 ..... 3 G5
  SBCH CW11 ..... 8 B3

V

Valebrook Dr NANT CW5 ..... 40 B5

Vale Gdns ALS/KID ST7 ..... 26 D3
Valley Cl ALS/KID ST7 ..... 25 G4
Valley Rd CW/HAS CW1 ..... 21 E5
Vauxhall Rd NANT CW5 ..... 29 F3
Verdin Ct CW/HAS CW1 ..... 11 F4
Vere St CW/HAS CW1 ..... 2 E1
Verity Cl CW/HAS CW1 ..... 23 F3
Vernon St CW/HAS * CW1 ..... 21 G2
Vernon Wy CW/HAS CW1 ..... 3 G1
Vicarage Gdns SBCH CW11 ..... 7 G1
Vicarage La SBCH CW11 ..... 7 H1
Vicarage Rd CW/HAS CW1 ..... 23 G1
Victoria Av CW/HAS CW1 ..... 23 F3
  CW/SHV CW2 ..... 21 E3
Victoria Mill Dr NANT CW5 ..... 30 C4
Victoria St CW/HAS CW1 ..... 3 F2
  SBCH CW11 ..... 8 B2
Villiers Russell Cl CW/HAS CW1 ..... 3 G1
Vincent St CW/HAS CW1 ..... 3 J3
Vine Tree Av CW/SHV CW2 ..... 2 D7
  CW/SHV CW2 ..... 31 G5
Volunteer Av NANT CW5 ..... 29 F4
Volunteer Flds NANT CW5 ..... 29 F4

W

Waine St CW/HAS CW1 ..... 22 A2
Waldron Gdns CW/SHV CW2 ..... 31 F1
Waldron Rd CW/HAS CW1 ..... 23 G4
Waldron's La CW/HAS CW1 ..... 11 H3
Walford Av CW/SHV CW2 ..... 2 C5
Walker Cl CW/HAS CW1 ..... 23 G3
Walkers La ALS/KID ST7 ..... 17 G2
Walker St CW/HAS CW1 ..... 21 G2
Wall Fields Cl NANT * CW5 ..... 29 F3
Wall Fields Rd NANT CW5 ..... 29 F3
Wallis St CW/HAS CW1 ..... 3 H2
Wall La NANT CW5 ..... 29 F4
Walpole Av CW/HAS CW1 ..... 23 F2
Walthall St CW/SHV CW2 ..... 2 E6
Wareham Dr CW/SHV CW2 ..... 11 G4
Warmingham La SBCH CW11 ..... 7 E1
Warmingham Rd CW/HAS CW1 ..... 11 H3
  SBCH CW11 ..... 8 A3
Warrington Av CW/HAS CW1 ..... 21 H1
Wasdale Gv CW/HAS CW1 ..... 11 G3
Watch La SBCH CW11 ..... 6 D3
Water-Lode NANT CW5 ..... 29 E5
Waterloo Rd CW/HAS CW1 ..... 23 G3
Waterside Ms SBCH CW11 ..... 14 A1
Waverton Av CW/SHV CW2 ..... 41 F3
Wayside Linley ALS/KID ST7 ..... 27 E5
Weaver Cl ALS/KID ST7 ..... 25 H4
  CW/HAS CW1 ..... 7 H2
Weaver Rd NANT CW5 ..... 29 F4
Weaverside NANT CW5 ..... 38 B3
Welland Cl SBCH CW11 ..... 7 H1
Well Bank SBCH CW11 ..... 8 C3
Wellcroft Cl CW/SHV CW2 ..... 31 G3
Wellesley Av CW/HAS CW1 ..... 23 F3
Welles St SBCH CW11 ..... 8 C2
Wellington Rd NANT CW5 ..... 38 B1
Well La ALS/KID ST7 ..... 26 B4
Wells Av CW/HAS CW1 ..... 23 G2
Wellswood Dr CW/SHV CW2 ..... 41 F3
Welshmen's La NANT CW5 ..... 28 D2
Welsh Rw NANT CW5 ..... 29 E5
Wesley Av ALS/KID ST7 ..... 26 C3
  SBCH CW11 ..... 8 C3
Wesley Cl NANT CW5 ..... 29 F5
Wesley Pl CW/SHV CW2 ..... 3 G6
Wessex Cl CW/SHV CW2 ..... 40 D2
West Av CW/HAS CW1 ..... 2 D2
  CW/SHV CW2 ..... 33 E5
Westbourne Av CW/HAS CW1 ..... 21 F1
Westbury Cl CW/SHV CW2 ..... 31 H1
Western Av NANT CW5 ..... 38 B2
Westfield Dr CW/SHV CW2 ..... 30 D2
Westgate Pk CW/SHV CW2 ..... 41 F3
Westhead Av ALS/KID ST7 ..... 26 D3
Westholme Cl CW/SHV CW2 ..... 31 H2
Westmere Cl CW/SHV CW2 ..... 33 E5
Westmere Ct CW/HAS * CW1 ..... 22 C5
Westmere Dr CW/HAS CW1 ..... 22 C5
Westminster St CW/SHV CW2 ..... 3 F5
Weston La CW/SHV CW2 ..... 32 A5
Weston Rd CW/HAS CW1 ..... 3 K7
  CW/HAS CW1 ..... 33 G2
West St CW/HAS CW1 ..... 2 D1
  CW/SHV CW2 ..... 23 F2
West Wy CW/SHV CW2 ..... 32 A5
  SBCH CW11 ..... 8 A5
Wettenhall Rd NANT CW5 ..... 18 C3
  NANT CW5 ..... 28 D1
Wharfdale Av CW/HAS CW1 ..... 11 G3
The Wharf CW/HAS * CW1 ..... 3 H2

Index - featured places

Notes